Saunas and War Toys

(or) By moose-back into darkest Caprolalia

Kalikiano Kalei

Aeolian Flights Press

SACRAMENTO, CALIFORNIA

Kalikiano Kalei/Aeolian Flights Publishing
5960 S. Land Park Drive, #256
Sacramento, CA 95822-3313 USA
www.webs.lanset.com/aeolusaero

Publisher's Note: This is a work of fiction. Names, characters, places, and incidents are a product of the author's imagination. Locales and public names are sometimes used for atmospheric purposes. Any resemblance to actual people, living or dead, or to businesses, companies, events, institutions, or locales is completely coincidental.

Book Layout © 2017 BookDesignTemplates.com

Saunas and War toys, Kalikiano Kalei. -- 1st ed.
ISBN 978-0-692-94059-4

Markku Makinen, educator, author, CBRN specialist, survivor of many Finnish flying moose intercepts, and very good personal friend.

"Patriotism has become a spiritual syphilis that devours the brains and grins out through empty eye sockets with moronic hate!".

—CARL NIELSEN, COMPOSER

Markku and Kalikiano with Satakunta Air Wing J-35 Draken.

Contents

Ch. 1. THE SWEDISH OPTION:

It has been brought to my attention innumerable times by well-meaning friends that vacations are principally intended for relaxation. Whether purely for a break from the normal work grind or simply to indulge in some quality time for one's self, the conventional wisdom suggests that holidays are best spent in an unstructured, relaxing environment-- preferably, if at all possible, in an exotic locale and surrounded by interesting sights, sounds and experiences.

Well, friends, I have managed to meet the last three criteria, even if the central thrust (no pun intended) of half a month of leave was recently dedicated to an exploration of defense and military concerns in the northern most regions of Europe. I have learned from previous experience to offer simple, uncomplicated and possibly dissembling answers when asked by acquaintances what I did on vacation. These usually consist of innocuous, bland recounting statements of how peacefully the palm trees waved on the beaches of Majorca, or how picturesque the white-washed cottages are on the Island of Mikonos. I usually don't tell them the truth--that I just spent a week catching up on the latest advances in chemical and biological warfare protection techniques, followed by a week-long Cook's Tour of Finland's military and aviation facilities. By setting this forth, I am breaking that precedent simply because those of you who know me know I am prone to some unique predilections, while those of you who don't could care less.

Every three years or so the Swedish National Defense Research Establishment (located in Umeå, and acronymically named FOA) conducts the world's largest and most respected international symposium on chemical and biological warfare protection technology in Stockholm. I have attended this conference since 1992, just after the Middle Eastern Gulf War had ended--the 4th such gathering since its inception. In view of the recent conclusion of Saddam Hussein's NBC threat, there was at that time a particularly keen world-wide interest in this normally somewhat obscure and exotic area of defense affairs.

I had planned to attend the symposium again this year in a nominal capacity as the sole "Saudi Arabian" delegate, although actually a United States citizen. Coincidentally, a very good Finnish friend and associate in chemical defense, living in Turku, had been after me for some time to visit his native country and spend some time taking in the Finnish national defense establishment as his guest. X, a former noncom in the Finnish chemical defense service, is now a respected writer on military topics and is also a teacher, with many ties to people in that country's defense forces. When I told him I would be spending a week in Stockholm at the FOA conference, X would not let me demure from his invitation to spend an extra week in Finland immediately thereafter. Obtaining the extra week was really no problem so I arranged to make the trip across the Gulf of Bothnia via ferry the day the Stockholm gathering ended. Upon hearing this, X, who is 35 but already a very interesting and capable individual with many talents, put together a stimulating agenda of activities for my consideration in advance of my visit--more of which shall be divulged shortly. [Have I ever been able to tell anything simply, bereft of complex and frequently completely unnecessary detail? Do pigs fly through the skies of Saudi Arabia? Does the Pope leave the Holy Toilet Seat up when he takes a Holy Whiz?].

The Scandinavian fortnight that ensued was a whirlwind of fascinating if highly technical and very condensed mucking about in Finnish defense matters. It was so highly structured that there really wasn't much that was relaxing about it, except that such activities are of remarkable interest to me and I am at my zenith doing such things. Although I was completely exhausted when I returned to Riyadh, there is no question in my mind that it was one of the most unusual and enjoyable experiences I have undertaken in the past 10 years.

The trip started off on 8 June with a British Airways flight from Riyadh to Heathrow, where a linking flight on the same carrier would take me to Stockholm's Arlanda Airport. SAS, normally the popular carrier for trips to the lands of the midnight sun, was on strike--a first for that established, reputable airline. The BA flight left King Khalid International Airport (Riyadh) at 0030 hours in the morning on what is popularly referred to as the "red eye flight." After struggling through the usual hassles clearing the Kingdom's passport and customs control and setting off the severely misadjusted metal detection system with the screws in my eyeglasses numerous time (a royal pain, assuredly, and caused by the extreme ineptitude of the Arab operators), I made it on board the flight. The new Boeing 767-100 was soon in the air and the flight to London was smooth and uneventful, if you exclude the noise of British celebrants attacking the alcohol stocks upon clearing Saudi airspace.

The makeover construction at Heathrow has been going on for several years now, but I was able to negotiate the bus transfer from Terminal One to Terminal Four without much trouble and was soon on my way to Stockholm after a short layover. Arrival on the Boeing 737-400 series aircraft occurred after just three hours, and the weather at Arlanda was just the way I am used to it (being an old San Franciscan): moderately high overcast with some hazy sunshine.

Ch. 2. STOCKHOLM AGAIN:

Catching the SKr 50 airport bus into Stockholm's massive central terminal, I was soon at the desk of the Hotel Wallin, which is conveniently a block away from the Norra Latin Conference Center where the FOA Symposium takes place, and near the Dröttningatan pedestrian mall. My wife was flying out to be with me, but perhaps due to the intervention of the *Tomptens*, her flight had been delayed and wouldn't be arriving until the afternoon of the next day. (The Tomptens, by the way, are mythical little people much like the Irish Leprechauns, dear to the hearts of the Scandinavians). Therefore, I had a day and a half in which to indulge myself with some explorations of Stockholm-- an aspect of my last trip to this city I had not had much time to engage in.

As usual, Stockholm was seemingly alive with amazingly healthy, robust, vigorous natives. It seemed as if everyone wore shorts and abbreviated summer attire despite the fact that the weather was intermittently rainy and cool for about half of the time I was there. Inquiring about this, I learned that the Scandinavian summer is a scarce and much appreciated commodity. Therefore, cool and windy or not, the hardy Swedes feel that "sidereal summer" mandates summer clothing, and disdain the frequently chilly draughts of fresh air that regularly sweep the Stockholm archipelago.

Of course, quite often the weather is beautiful and sunny, but overall the weather of Stockholm is not all that different from that of the American Pacific Northwest in that rain, fog and cold breezes are constant companions in summer months. In 1992 the Swedish nation was experiencing a record heat wave and there was nothing but sun and languid June warmth throughout the FOA conference held in that year. What a contrast this year's conference was! It rained & thundered the second day I was there with a ferocity that impressed me. My 1992 experience with balmy weather had misled me into leaving my umbrella at home, so my first foray was taken to find one. Fortunately, a local Seven-Eleven convenience store (yes, they have them in Stockholm) provided one for SKr 66, and I remained armed with this (disposable) bumbershoot until I was ready to board the ferry for Finland.

Stockholm certainly has to be one of the most beautiful of the world's capital cities, as any person who has strolled leisurely along its quays in summer warmth will readily tell you. The Swedes, being an active, outdoorsy people, delight in walking and cycling; accordingly, much of the city has been planned to accommodate these activities. Additionally, with a history which dates back several hundred years, much of the interesting architecture has been preserved in the older areas. In some districts, more recent structures built in the 20s and 30s predominate, all interesting examples of the edificial styles of that prewar era, but most of the city has been built to accommodate scenic inducement to foot traffic. The heart of the original settlement, Gamla Stan, has been preserved on its island as a living museum, with shops, businesses and restaurants. The sidewalk cafés of Stockholm, at least in warm summery weather, absolutely wonderful. As a life-long, inveterate cappuccino-sipper. Of course, in summer hordes of tourists descend upon the Swedish capitol, bent on sightseeing and vicarious enjoyment of the city's attractions. Sooner or later this urban congestion grates a bit on the nerves, no matter how pleasant the surroundings are. It didn't escape me that I was far more aware of this aspect of the city on this trip than I was on my first visit, and after a week of elbowing crowds on the main pedestrian thoroughfares I was more than ready to make a break for Finland's less densely populated shores.

Ch. 3. THE LATEST IN DEATH & DESTRUC-
TION:

My wife finally arrived, her flight on BA through Heathrow from San Francisco (polar route) being a bit further delayed by connection complications. It wasn't a whole lot of fun, waiting outside the arrival gates at Arlanda, owing to the crowds present on similar business but I managed to snag a Swedish magazine to keep myself amused for several hours until she walked into the lounge and we were able to catch the shuttle into Stockholm.

For her the week was pretty much open time, with most of her days spent sightseeing and becoming a bit more familiar with the city of Stockholm (this was her first visit). My own time was pretty solidly filled up from the 11th through the 16th with the chemical and biological defense technology sessions of the conference, in which all the latest advances in protection against NBC death and destruction were explored, papers delivered, specialty briefings held, and collective and individual protection equipment exhibited.

Probably the single most interesting aspect of this particular conference was the latest informational assessment of the recent Japanese Sarin gas incident, in which the *Aum Shinrikyo* Cult released this deadly nerve agent against civilians in the Tokyo subways. Attending the conference to deliver an official technical report on the events and subsequent findings was Dr. Prof. Kazuhiko Maekawa of Tokyo University Hospital. Professor Maekawa presented a fairly adequate overview of all that had taken place, including a detailed accounting of measures which had been initiated to meet the threat and provide aid to the victims. The overall reception from the delegates was that the information was still not specific enough to be as helpful as might have been preferred, but the subject of related concerns centering on use of these deadly nerve agents as terrorist weapons was thoughtfully explored to everyone's satisfaction. The consensus over the Japanese presentation was that Japan had been truly caught by surprise and was largely unprepared for such a possibility as this attack taking place in a densely populated urban district. One of the most revealing findings to emerge was that due to the unexpectedly rare nature of massive organophosphate poisoning taking place in a non-rural, metropolitan center, the diagnosis and treatment of the injuries arising was severely impeded. Therefore, it was far less effective and expeditious than it might have been had the causative nature been suspected from the onset. many other details of the incident were released, some of which were still marginally classified, but suffice to say it was quite a source of interest for all the symposium delegates.

The next most interesting item on the FOA chemical protection symposium agenda concerned the latest updates on UNSCOM's efforts in Iraq to destroy the Iraqi "weapons of mass destruction." I personally dislike that popular press-promulgated phrase, but what the hell. UN spokesman Rolf Ekeus presented a briefing on the 1992 through 1995 activities of the munitions disposal teams and revealed along with other information that Iraq was already starting to show significant evidence of clandestinely developing a precursor base for a new covert biological weapons program. He stated that almost all of the existing stockpiles of chemical-filled munitions (SCUD type warheads, 122mm rocket and 155mm artillery projectiles filled with mustard and nerve agents) had been satisfactorily destroyed; the slide and video presentations which accompanied his talk were quite interesting, as well. As for the vaunted Iraqi "Baby Milk Factory," the bombing of which was so heavily propagandised by the Iraqis during the war, it was conclusively identified as having contained a Sarin and GV nerve agent processing plant within its site. The Al Muthana CBW facility, Iraq's largest and chief CBW manufacturing and storage site (located south of Baghdad), had been rendered useless and had now been turned back over to Iraq with an elaborate video and sensor surveillance system installed to monitor future use of the site. Still further remarks were directed towards the future prospects of cheaply made biologicals being developed by Iraq, since weapons of this type are far less complicated in terms of their design, manufacture and storage requirements.

Other segments of the symposium's agenda dealt with the increasing possibility of further non-national (i.e. non-state-aligned terrorist organisations) use of chemical and especially biological agents, after the Tokyo model. Steps being taken by the world-wide CBW community to deal with this prospect were reviewed. Although the recent movie thriller Outbreak, featuring Dustin Hoffman, exaggerates the potential of such a problem for cinematic effect, quite a bit of sober thoughtfulness was produced by the film, heightening popular awareness of biological agents as weapons of war. It seems the UN chemical weapons convention (CWC) is pretty much on the road towards bring about an end to the proliferation of chemical weapons, world-wide, but the corresponding convention to control biological weapons isn't faring as well. Much disagreement among nations as to definitions, terminology, structure of the act, and unresolved issues involving implementation, remains. We might non-unreasonably expect the next major international threat to come from covert use of these biological weapons, since they are far more easily prepared, transported, cultivated and stored than their chemical counterparts--far more so, and in smaller but vastly more lethal quantities. The practical bottom line would seem to be (tongue in cheek, but not very far)...from an expatriate traveler's viewpoint...to stick to using only bottled water on trips abroad until further notice.

Luminaries, dignitaries and other CBW worthies present at this premier symposium included the head of the English Porton Down CBW establishment and the equivalent counterparts from numerous countries around the world (over 60 nations participated). The Swedish Minister of Defense opened the conference and the new US NBC "Czar," Dr. Theodore Prociv, brought the attendees up to date on the recent reshuffling of US defense department NBC logistics (attributable more to the harsh economic realities forced upon the US armed forces than by a desire to be more effectively organised, I would imagine). There were many similar briefings and papers presented, more research studies detailed, and the usual small private conferences held on stair-landings between sessions. Attending nations from the Middle East included the Iranians, Egyptians and Kuwaitis (the burned child fears the fire), but with Saudi Arabia's capitol, Riyadh, only 212 kms from the Iraqi chemical threat in 1991, guess what wealthy Arab nation didn't put in an appearance? The fact that I attended made me the sole "token" delegate from Saudi Arabia, although I was not attending in any official capacity therein. Many of the other symposium delegates were puzzled to see what appeared to be a fair-skinned, blonde and green-eyed "Arab" representing that nation, providing me with great amusement.

Among the non-technical items on the agenda was the official welcoming ceremony for the symposium delegates hosted in the spectacular Stockholm City Hall by the Mayor. The Stockholm City Hall is an immense, soaring, red brick architectural wonder in which the yearly Nobel Peace Prizes are presented, among other things. The welcoming speech was followed by a huge buffet smorgasbord, consisting of table after table of traditional foods, wines, smoked salmon, caviar, etc., while delegates enjoyed a few hours of social diversion in the city hall's great reception room.

Ch. 4. OOPS...THERE GOES THE VASA, YOUR MAJESTY!

Other events of note on the symposium agenda included a bus tour of the greater environs of Stockholm, and a very special evening diner cruise of the 22,000+ island Stockholm archipelago, held on two old Swedish steam-powered vessels of the early 1900s. The dinner was excellent, of course, consisting of traditional Swedish cuisine, and it was great fun to stand up on the upper decks watching the scenic coastlines of the various islands pass in the perpetual twilight of the Swedish summer evening. The nature of the protracted evening-like ambience which is characteristic of the far northern longitudes, makes such outings very romantic by nature--the effect is not unlike enjoying a sunset for several hours. This fact is not lost on Swedish couples, who may be seen leisurely walking along the seaside long into the night, and our three-hour dinner cruise, although it ended at 11 PM, seemed to take place in a sort of 5PM time-warp. Only after midnight does the sun dip below the horizon, and then only for an hour or two. The effect of this is interesting, but it takes a bit of getting used to by non-native tourists.

As the week's events unfolded, more opportunities occurred for recreational sightseeing amidst the seriousness of the symposium's agenda. One such "don't miss this" activity was a tour of the extremely interesting VASA museum. The VASA, a magnificent royal 17th century wooden hulled ship of the line which was especially commissioned by King

Gustav Vaasa as his flagship, ingloriously capsized and sank not far from its construction site almost immediately after it was launched in 1633. This 300-year-old singular example of nautical architecture of that period remained at the bottom of the Stockholm harbor in 40 meters of water almost completely forgotten--owing to the vast embarrassment suffered by the King--until the early 1960s, at which time a massive and costly effort was made to recover it. Due to the combination of extremely cold water (almost devoid of oxygen) and thick, tar-like mud found on the bottom of the harbor, the vessel was preserved almost entirely intact for three centuries; when it was rediscovered and salvage attempts made to retrieve it, the world was amazed to find substantially as it was in that distant time when it had gone down.

The 300-ton royal baroque masterpiece of maritime engineering sank in virtually calm conditions, taking 18 men down with it, due to its being overly top-heavy and under-ballasted. The gun ports were a mere 4.5 feet above the waterline, partly the result of the King having ordered that an additional gun-deck be built which had not been on the original design plan, and when a slight gust caught the ship's sails right after launch, it immediately heeled over and went down. Recent study has been shown that the ship as built could not sustain more than a 10-degree list without encountering disaster such as that which overtook it! Fortunately, a multi-million Kroner restoration project begun in the early 1960s, after the ship was brought up, has resulted in this amazingly preserved ship that is now permanently housed in the VASA museum. It remains one of the most interesting sights which can be seen in Stockholm, and stands alone as the sole surviving example of a 17th century capital ship in the whole world. The King's extreme consternation in 1633 was understandable; fortunately for all of us today, this accident of history has contributed spectacularly to our understanding of 17th century Swedish maritime technology.

At any rate, the brooding bulk of the VAASA'S dark hull is an awesome sight as it emerges in the darkened, carefully controlled environment of the special building wherein she is housed. As the eyes become adjusted to the lowered light, the stupendous size of this behemoth creates an impression that is hard to forget.

Ch. 5. MEETING THE FINNISH CONTINGENT:

The symposium did not host a formal dinner this time at the Swedish Military Academy, as it had in 1992, so the elegant black-silk-with-gold trim Cheong Sam dress I had had my wife bring along with her did not get its evening of splendorous display. I continued to hear small muted mutterings of discontent over having brought it along for nothing all week, albeit just slightly out of my range of hearing, and I did sympathise with her for having had to lug it carefully half-way around the world with her just to keep it on a hanger.

Meanwhile I was busy meeting various delegates and encountering a few of the Finnish contingent who would later host my visit to that country's defense installations. These included the Commandant of the Finnish NBC Protection School and his aide, the Chief Scientist of the Finnish Defense Research Agency (whose son is a Finnish Air Force Draken pilot), the Manager of the Kemira Oy Company (NBC products), and two Finnish Air Force representatives (the Commander of the Satakunta Air Wing, and a Major from the Finnish Air Force Academy).

This was really my first contact with the Finns, aside from my friend X, and I was struck by their characteristic national personality--explained to me by our Finnish cardiac cath lab nurse colleague in Riyadh. There is an old joke about the Finns, apparently, that goes something like this: "When the

Finns go to a formal function, they dress seriously, act seriously, and look serious; when they attend an informal gathering, they dress semi-formally, act casually, and look serious; when they go to a party, they dress casually, act silly, and look serious." In all seriousness, I later was to find out far more about this interesting nature while visiting Finland, and found them to be very, very delightful and warm-hearted people, despite their frequently dour initial appearance.

Meanwhile, the Swedish conference continued. The cost of everything in Sweden in 1995 was quite steep, compared to 1992 (it wasn't cheap then, either), with the exchange rate being about 1US$ = 7.1 SKr. Despite being an expatriate used to using different monetary units from several countries, it was quite easy to go through Kroner like play money. A Chinese dinner I hosted for 7 colleagues in the Gamla Stan old city cost just under a thousand Kroner! Perhaps not much by Tokyo or Hong Kong standards, but a whole lot for this middle-class American. Alcoholic beverages (wines and beer) are quite expensive, with spirits (hard liquor) even more so. Even the usual touristy souvenirs and kitschy gifts are quite pricey. Hand crafted folk-art such as the famous Red Pony, and more elegant items like world-famous Matts Ohlen crystal sculptures are even more so. Swedish and Finnish crystal and porcelains are expensive enough in their nations of origin, but even more so outside them, so some expensive purchases are almost mandatory.

I settled for several expensive, but masterfully hand carved, wooden figurines by Gunarsson, a well-known Stockholm artist. Two of the three figures were of a young male and female student, dressed in the customary attire of successful graduates of university exams (the white topped, visored student cap and silver-knobbed walking cane that are the traditional regalia of graduation). They are quite skillfully executed and a delight to behold, but I have always been interested in the old student customs of Europe and Scandinavia so these were especially meaningful to me. At about US$ 90 each, they were costly, but well worth the cost as several of the few souvenirs I took home with me from my trip.

Ch. 6. LARS LARSSON, CALL HOME:

Something that caught my attention and interest was the proliferation of cellular phones of the ultra-small pocket variety on the streets, which seem to have swept the Scandinavian countries like wild-fire. Everywhere you look on the streets of Stockholm, you find the characteristic hand growing out of the ear that marks the cell-phone user. Mothers, businessmen, teenagers, street drunks, even children. Everyone had the small cellular phone holster at the hip, and aside from constituting an obvious sign of trendy status, they appear to be as common as personal pagers were in the USA recently. A taxi driver told me that cell phones are very, very inexpensive in Scandinavia (Finland's Nokia Company is a major player in this market, making small, precise electronic items such as these that compete head-on with the best products Japan turns out). It was amusing seeing this new visible symbol of contemporary world communications progress making such inroads in Sweden. Personally, as an individual who absolutely hates, loathes, despises, abominates and otherwise can't stand telephonic communications devices (I've been on hospital call for too many years like these things, and especially "beepers"), I wouldn't be caught any other way than dead with one of them. It is bad enough to be tied into the telephonic network by day in an occupational context, but I regard my "off-time' as sacrosanct. Telephones really tighten my jaws, since they are such annoyingly patent violations of personal privacy and peaceful harmony.

Another observation garnered on this visit to Stockholm was the fact that Swedish women all seem to
be...and they can be no other suitable word for it
other than simply...*healthy.* I don't think I have seen
more tightly toned, well-conditioned clustered in
one place than in Sweden. Even the non-Scandina-
vian immigrants in Sweden's capitol appear to be
more body-conscious (in excellent shape) there
than in their native countries. I was greatly impressed by the great abundance of well-shaped
gastrocs and gluteii, and women on the street
seemed all to have beautiful long legs that extended from their chins downwards to their ankles.
Very few overweight or poorly conditioned people in
evidence, as far as I could see. Not certain how it is
out in the country, but I would bet that obesity is not
a common problem in rural Sweden, either.

Although there wasn't a lot of time left between
events to explore the culinary aspects of Stockholm, my wife and I did manage to sample a
restaurant or two on evening strolls. One of these
was an uninspiring Chinese eatery that promised
more than it appeared to offer, and another was the
somewhat well-known disco called SAIGON, which
is a sand-bagged and bunkered bar/café with a
subterranean disco floor featuring songs of the Vietnam era. Most of the kids hanging around in it
weren't even born when that war was going on, but
I can't blame them for being interested in the image
in view of the importance of Stockholm's rep as a
major refuge for peaceniks, US military deserters
and anti-war protestors in the 60s and 70s. I was
reminded that I had briefly considered deserting the
US Air Force to fly to Sweden, while on duty in the

US ZI, back in 1968. But for a change of heart I could now be living in Sweden as one of the Vietnam peace movement refugees of 30 years ago. Life has an interesting and frequently ironic way of imparting reflection and insight into one's life, as the trail through it continues.

All things eventually end, of course, and so the 5th FOA International Chemical Agent Symposium wound down with the usual informal business contacts and sessions that spring up during coffee breaks and social hours. The Chinese (PRC) delegates were looking forward to hosting a CBW medical conference in Beijing in 1997; that would be something to attend, since the Beijing Chemical Defense Research Institute would be hosting it and there is much to do and see in China. In 1996 the next medical treatment of chemical warfare injuries symposium (CBMTS-2) would take place in Switzerland, hosted by the Swiss National Defense Research Laboratories; this is on the doorstep of the Bernese Oberland and a stone's throw from Eiger, on the western end of the Thunnersee that brackets InterLaken.

Ch. 7. WHERE PRECISELY DID THE ESTONIA SINK?

Came the 16th of June and it was time to pack up. I attended last minute conferences and some steering committees for future conferences, and then we were on our way to the Viking Ferry terminal where we would catch the massive, ocean-going ship they euphemistically call a "ferry boat." Our passage was to take us across the Gulf of Bothnia to the ancient Finnish city of Turku (called Åbo in Swedish, owing to the role Sweden has played in Finland's past history). The cost for this 10 hour) journey through the Swedish archipelago to Finland was about US$ 300 for two. It was, however, quite a unique trip and we had a private cabin much the same as one would have on a real ocean voyage, despite the relative brevity of the trip. The route is very heavily traveled by both Swedes and Finns, and many make the trip without booking a cabin; large numbers of softly padded reclining chairs on the inner promenade decks make this possible. Having had to live out of suitcases for well over a week already, my wife and I were both keen on having the chance to catch some quiet, undisturbed sleep, and the luxury of a shower was not lost on us either. After spending the first 4 hours of the trip on deck watching the silent islands glide by, I turned in and slept soundly until we were within an hour of landfall in Turku.

On board, the ferry were almost all of the Finnish delegates, including those previously referenced, and one of their number found us not long after we had boarded and invited us to attend a midnight buffet with them. I was fairly well done in by all the activity of the previous week and so declined, preferring to invest in some solid sleep; still, it was a very nice gesture that set the tone for the rest of the week in Finland. As it turned out, I would need the extra hours of sleep later.

The ferry we were on, named the Amarello, was about the size of a small to medium off-shore cruise liner, averaging about 3000+ tons displacement. It was very similar to the ill-fated Estonia, formerly of the Siila Lines, which had sunk off the coast of Finland the previous winter. The Estonia was fitted with what are called roll-on/roll-off loading doors, meaning that it had automobile access doors both in the bow as well as the stern. Our ship, and most of the more recent Viking and Siila Lines ships, are now fitted either with stern-only doors or have their bow doors permanently welded shut. It was apparently a malfunctioning latch on the visor-like bow door of the Estonia which allowed the rough seas to enter the cargo deck, flooding it enough to allow a severe disturbance in balance to occur which caused the ship to sink. Since the loss of the Estonia, full safety revisions of the designs have been undertaken, and the rear-only door design such as that which we were on was considered quite safe. Of further significance was the fact that the seas in the Bothnian Gulf are quite serene in the summer, while they are often unusually rough during the winter months. All in all, our trip over was smooth and pleasant--a unique excursion that I would recommend to anyone considering a similar trip to Finland from Sweden.

The morning of arrival in Turku we followed some of the Finnish delegates off the ship and were met by my friend X and his wife. I had never met X, despite several years of close contact via phone, letter and fax. Despite our unfamiliarity with each other, X and his wife spotted us and took us in tow, driving us back to their modern flat in the suburbs of this most ancient of Finland's cities. X and his wife are not actually married in any ordinary sense of the word, but live together as husband and wife might; this common law arrangement seems to be an unremarkable Finnish social convention. They are wonderfully hospitable people who, although a bit younger than my wife and I, took us into their homes as if we were long lost cousins returning after a prolonged separation. X's wife is a supervisor with one of the largest and most well-known of the Finnish candy manufacturing firms, the Leaf Company. As a result, we were continually supplied with every type of candy, gum, confection, and Xylitol-sweetened product one could imagine, throughout the duration of our week in Finland. The Finns are particularly fond of Anise-flavored candies and consume great amounts of licorice. Unfortunately, licorice has the effect of being bad for those with blood pressure problems, but this doesn't seem to deter consumption of it in that country. Some Finnish specialties, such as one called Salmiakki take a bit of getting used to, but most Finnish candies are excellent. It goes almost without saying that I managed to eat my way through most of these things without any difficulty during the week, and also brought back a quantity of them to Riyadh.

As soon as we had arrived at X's home, we were plied with the customary mid-afternoon groaning board of small snacks, sandwiches, cakes, biscuits and cheeses (the Finns eat well, and frequently; in the winter, it helps to keep them going through the severe cold). I had brought two bottles of costly spirits with me as a gift for X, knowing how expensive they are in Finland; imagine my chagrin when I discovered that neither X nor his wife drink alcohol-- surely an exception to the rule in a country where drinking is usually considered a pleasant social custom. The bottle of 15-year-old aged single malt (Laphroaig, from the Isle of Islay) and a bottle of Chateau Neuf Du Pape Rhône wine were politely put aside without much further ado. I guess you can't get it right every time, can you?

The first day in Finland (native word: Suomi) was spent taking a closer look at X's remarkable reference library and collection of chemical defense respirators. He has the only other collection as large as my own that I am aware of. Now, most people will hardly be expected to go into paroxysms of delight over a heap of old moldering rubber and canvas gasmasks, but to a specialist in this sort of thing some of his acquisitions are truly unique. He has an example of one of the earliest Russian WWI protective masks, known as the 1916 Selinski-Kummandt mask; this was a design that set the style for most succeeding Russian designs and featured a rubber over-the-head hood fitted with a charcoal canister on a connecting tube. I won't bore those of you who could care less about historic developments in chemical warfare respirator design and further, but this is simply one example of some of his interesting and historic specimens. His reference library is also quite broad and comprehensive, dealing with many aspects of military history and chemical warfare. Before I was able to tear myself away from his study that first day, X had presented me with 5 or 6 somewhat rare and hard to get Finnish specimens of mask, which I had to have sent back to the US by post, in view of luggage limitations.

Early the next morning the small Toyota hatchback was loaded up with our luggage (X's and mine) and we began a 250-km trip north to the seaport city of Vaasa (Vaasa in Swedish), where an invitation had been extended to us to take a tour through the Kemira Oy Safety Products factory. Director Y would meet us there, and after the tour of this historic old facility where modern Finnish Army chemical warfare respirators and civilian counterparts are produced, we would stay the night at accommodations paid for by the company.

My wife and X's wife would spend the next few days traveling about Finland separately, seeing interesting sights, while X and I began our "military sight-seeing tour" of some of Finland's defense installations.

The drive to Vaasa was scenic and relaxing for someone such as myself, unfamiliar with Finland's gently rolling, alternating hectares of forest and farmland. We stopped whenever the urge hit for coffee at one of the roadside "Kioski," which are the Finnish equivalent of the small roadside snack concession and café. Finns, I found out, have a passion for coffee that is strong and full-bodied, and as a life-long addict of the full-strength article this national trait endeared these people all the more to me. Here and there along the route to Vaasa we passed a few quaintly rustic little cafés with considerable ambience all their own. One in particular featured a wonderful old windmill and a millpond sheltered by trees in which lived a manic family of ducks. Sitting there in the shade and enjoying the cool breezes, I could have lingered there all day.

The weather was sunny overall as we traveled northwest, but high scattered clouds--typical I was told of the Finnish summer--were not usually far from the horizon, bringing rain and drizzle to keep the trees moist. The sights along the road were picturesque, with the archetypal Finnish country home seeming to consist of a small cottage that is invariably painted a dull red or bright golden yellow. So uniform was this alternating color scheme that you were hard pressed to find any other color employed as exterior paint on dwellings. To be sure it created a colorful backdrop, set amidst the green forested areas and small interspersed fields of wheat and grain products which characterise the Finnish landscape in the western part of the nation.

Ch. 8. KEMIRA OY SAFETY PRODUCTS:

We took most of the morning to reach Vaasa, on the Bothnian Gulf coast. There we met the Director of the Kemira Oy Safety products, who is a blonde, rosy-cheeked fellow of small stature but immense presence. He brought us onto the grounds of the old Kemira Chemical Plant and gave us a tour of the historical buildings which have long occupied the site. The Safety Products division is part of the world-renown Kemira Chemical Company. The tour of the respirator and protective filter area was, of course, of special interest to us; the new Finnish Armed Forces M-95 respirator is now in production there, replacing the previous long-serving Finnish M-61/76 version of the American 1950s vintage M-9 mask. This new military respirator is a unique and innovative design, and one of the newest most advanced designs in use among military forces today.

The Kemira grounds are built on what was once the old Finnish Army Chemical Depot, a facility that goes back to days when it served as a conventional arsenal (late 1800s). Until recent years, the Kemira Company was a fully state-owned concern. In 1983, they went public and are now a 40% private stock owned corporation, as is the case with many of Finland's formerly nationalised industries. Interestingly, Finland is a sparsely populated nation with a total population of only about 5 million persons. The nation itself comprises a considerable geographic area aligned north and south, similar to Sweden and Norway in their shapes. Surprisingly, everyone seems to know everyone else, or so it would seem as the nation is a very close-knit one. In school, the Finns are required to learn at least one foreign language in addition to their native language and Swedish. This usually turns out to be English, although German is the usual alternative in view of historic ties to Germany in past decades. Finland was for centuries a Swedish territory, and during the first part of the Second World War it aligned itself with Nazi Germany against the Soviets; Russia was, apparently, the worst of two distasteful alternatives at the time, and Finns still harbor a lingering traditional animosity towards the Russians.

Most young Finns in their 20s speak excellent English, and most of those in their 30s and 40s speak it adequately, if not perfectly. Thus, getting along in Finland's major urban areas is not challenging at all for English speaking visitors. This is not the case at all in many of the more isolated rural areas, such as Lapland in the north.

That afternoon, after finishing the tour of Kemira Oy's facilities, their director took us to a charming little seaside restaurant he frequents for a sumptuous afternoon supper; then, at the nearby marina, he took us to his small covered power cruiser's dock for a two-kilometer trip to his private island. His cottage sits on the island commanding a panoramic vista, and nearby the main building is his sauna. I knew that sooner or later I would be introduced to this most characteristic of Finnish customs, and sure enough it wasn't long before we were enjoying the first of many such sessions throughout the week.

Ch. 9.THE ESSENTIAL FINNISH
EXPERIENCE...SAUNA:

The Finnish sauna comes in several varieties. There is the conventional sauna, known to most westerners, in which one sits in a birch or redwood lined room, splashing water on an electric or gas-fired stone hearth. Each dipperful of water creates clouds of very hot steam which increases the heat in the small enclosure until you are forced to momentarily seek relief by exiting and diving into the nearest body of cold water. In the case of the Kemira director's sauna, this was the Gulf of Bothnia itself, and take it from me--it was COLD! Then there is what is known as the smoke sauna. This is a special type of sauna in which both heat and smoke figure into the equation. Sessions in this variety of sauna include a further embellishment--the use of swatches of birch leaves to slap your skin (no, we're not talking some unusual form of Finnish S&M, here--it's actually quite refreshing).

Cold beer and small snacks are taken intermittently, sometimes afterwards, and as we sat around and swatted the king-sized Finnish mosquitoes, I learned some of the Lore of Finnish Sauna. One very important misunderstanding by many westerners is that saunas are used occasionally for sexual liaisons. Nothing could be further from the truth: sex and saunas are mutually incompatible. This was explained to me in this manner: "You can use a sauna to give birth to a baby, but it is against the custom to make them there." The fact is that saunas have been used for ages by Finnish women to deliver infants, but it would be a severe transgression of the tradition to use them for coital hanky-panky. I explained to our friend the Kemira director how this would be puzzling to the average Californian, who through fuzzy misconception associates hot tub sex encounters with anything remotely resembling a sauna and doubtless fueled with vast quantities of alcohol at that. Our Kemira director friend was clearly aghast at the very idea of the California custom!

At any rate, the sauna took place quite late but since it is still very light at 10PM in the north, that was not a problem. What was a problem was that first dive into the cold, cold water of the Gulf after having heated ourselves up to nearly 100 degrees centigrade by all that steam. The other two had no hesitation and dived straight off the floating dock into the frigid water, but I used the ladder and eased down into the icy fluid. This was clearly the wrong way to do it, as I found out later, but I was concerned that I would end up experiencing the equivalent of a hypothermically induced orchiotomy. Amazingly, my voice did not rise two octaves as the water reached the critical perineal plimsol line. I finally was able to ease all the way down into the bay and made a brave effort to swim a few strokes to a nearby buoy and back. I am sure the others could hear my teeth chattering each foot of the way, and it was quite a relief to get out of the water after that bit of *buck-nekked* frivolity, I can assure you.

One of the wonderful things about the traditional Finnish sauna is the sense of equality that obtains while taking this steaming ritual. All men are considered equal in the sauna; when you enter that steaming room together you are all brothers, after a fashion. It wouldn't matter if you were in there with the President of the nation and the local town drunk--while enjoying this ancient, honorable custom, all are equals in the sight of whatever Norse gods still inhabit the frigid forests of the northlands. Although unrelated men and women don't usually take mixed saunas in groups anymore, married couples and close friends still enjoy saunas together, and only the poorest, most wretchedly impoverished Finns lack a sauna adjacent to their homes. Corporations provide them for their workers, cooperative and apartment complexes maintain them for renters, and even Finnish military forces have them in their barrack areas. Sauna is the essential Finnish experience.

The sense of mutual bonding you experience in the sauna is a cathartically primal one--verging somewhere along the lines of a Robert Bly Male Consciousness Session and an ancient Moose post-hunt tribal ritual. This first sauna was for me such an experience and the Finns seem to delight in introducing newcomers to their ancient practice. Fortunately, these days visitors are politely asked if they care to share the experience, rather than simply being hauled off to the sauna as was frequently the case years ago. The Finns take their sauna seriously, and fortunately I am an adventurous person by inclination and rarely turn down an opportunity to experience something unique for the

first time. By the time my week in Finland was concluded, I had developed a profound and genuine
appreciation for this custom.

The Finns also have a very healthy regard for their
bodies, and are not seemingly burdened with all the
latent Christian guilt associated with nakedness that
is frequently a product of Western religious tradition. It is sometimes hard for them to understand
the sort of excessive modesty or obsessive lewdity
that are frequently component by-products of religious guilt in North America. In this bodily sense of
self, they are very healthy people, even if their national diet is high in saturated fats and full of
unhealthy cholesterols.

It had been a full day in the Vaasa area, and we
turned in somewhat late that night. The Finns are
used to staying up well past midnight in the summer
months, due to the perpetual light--something that
was to prove to be a distinct irritation for me, since I
need a solid 8 hours of sleep every night regardless
of whether it is still light or not. We were well fed,
scourged and I for one was so ready for sleep that
not even the legions of bird-sized mosquitoes could
keep me awake. Speaking of these pests, although
they are an omnipresent feature in Finland's lower
regions, around the lakes and plentiful water bodies, they seemed to be fairly slow and lumbering
things compared to their common North American
relatives. It was easy to swat them and score
strikes against them due to their deficit airspeed
and maneuvering ability, but their sheer numbers
make any sort of effective air defense against them
effort intensive. To be sure, the variety found in

northern Finland (Lapland) are a whole different breed, and are not only large and plentiful, but fast and ravenous as well. They compare, I think, to those found in Alaska and the Canadian Northwest Territories, which any canoe-portaging traveler will tell you are downright nasty little buggers.

Ch. 10. INTRODUCTION TO A FINNISH DRAGON:

Next day we traveled back to the Vaasa marina by boat and loaded up X's small Toyota hatch-back, saying good-bye to the Kemira director and thanking him for his excellent hospitality. Our next objective lay southwards towards the Central Finland Regional Air Defense Center, and the Satakunta Air Wing which operated at Tampere Air Base. We reached the Wing's perimeter just in time to meet the base's Deputy Commander who was to be our host for this segment of the tour. Although we had been told that it was possible that we would be given orientation flights in one of the Wing's new BAE Mk.51 Hawk jet trainers, we were surprised to learn that something a bit more exotic had been provided for this experience flying with the Finnish Air Force. The Deputy Commander took us to the operations building at the base and we went directly into a pre-flight emergency procedure orientation & training session for the Swedish built, two seat version of the SAAB J-35 Draken fighter. The J-35 Draken (Dragon) is a Mach 1.5 capable, delta-winged air defense fighter that the Finns have built under license and used for nearly 30 years. Despite its age (the design is more than 40 years old, and squadrons of them have been in use in Sweden for 4 decades now), it is still something of a marvelous aircraft to fly, sharing many common characteristics with the Mach 2 Convair F106A Delta Dart that we used to fly from Minot AFB in North Dakota back in the 60s. I was, as we used to say in the California surfing culture of my youth, "stoked!" The two-seat tandem version of the Draken is used for transition training and flight proficiency checks, and as with the two-seat tandem version of the Convair F106A, the two seat Draken could operate with virtually the same level of offensive capability as the single-seat version. The Satakunta Air Wing, responsible for all air defense operations for central Finland, flew a squadron of these beautiful old but capable birds, and a further squadron of the newer (subsonic) Hawk trainers.

The Draken in 1995 was just celebrating its 40th year of continuous service as an operational air-craft, the design having been first developed back in the 1950s. In fact, while at the FOA symposium the week before, I just missed being able to attend the annual Swedish Air Force air show, at which the 4th decade of Draken service was being cele-brated. At any rate, X and I spent the better part of the early afternoon being instructed and briefed on the finer points of emergency egress from a stricken Draken, using the excellent SAAB de-signed ejection seat the Draken is fitted with. The Finnish Air Force flies, in addition to the Draken and the Hawk, Russian built MiG-21Fbis fighters, alt-hough these operate at the Karelian Air Wing base in the east of the country and not at Satakunta. This complicates the task of Finnish Air Force life-sup-port technicians in that they must set up and maintain technical support services for at least 3 to 4 different types of egress systems (Russian, Swe-dish, British and American). The Hawks and the new US designed McDonnell-Douglas F/A-18 Hor-nets (which are being introduced to replace the Draken) both use the English Martin-Baker Mk.10L aircrew escape systems. The Draken uses an ear-lier but quite substantially developed Swedish escape system, and the MiGs use a completely al-together different Russian ejection system and matching personal equipment. Not an easy task when you consider that most Air Forces standard-ise on a single uniform system and only have to worry about servicing one type of egress equipment and component escape technology.

The Swedes, incidentally, were among the first to develop emergency ejection seat systems for mili-tary aircraft, and for many years it was thought that a Swedish pilot was the first to actually use such a system to leave his crippled aircraft in the early 50s, until never-before-released information surfaced about German World War Two efforts. The revela-tions indicated that a German pilot had in fact successfully made an emergency ejection at a far earlier date (in the 1940s), and until the Allies brought Germany to its knees in 1945 the Germans were actually the world's leaders in pioneering such escape technology. With the collapse of Ger-many's aviation industry, Sweden and England assumed the lead in this relatively new field of sur-vival technology.

SAAB, known to most Americans for their automo-biles, was originally founded to build aircraft and SAAB ejection systems are excellent. The Deputy Commander of the Satakunta Air Wing confided to me during our tour that in over 30 years of opera-tional use of the Draken, the SAAB seat had never had to be used; ironically, several months after I left Finland, the Finnish Air Force sustained its first crash of a Draken jet fighter in an accident. Unfortunately, the pilot did not survive the crash, but it was not the SAAB ejection seat that had failed, and the crash had not been a survivable one. This compares to a number of the *Mig-21F bis* fighters which have been lost regularly over the years. Apparently, the Drakens, despite their age, are well built and are undoubtedly superbly maintained for having served so long with so few problems. X and I were heartened to hear of the excellent safety record of the Finnish license-produced Draken, needless to say.

The egress briefing consisted of several hours of instruction, lecture and drill in emergency escape procedures. Instructor pilot: "If something happens that requires emergency ejection you will hear me say in a loud, clear voice EJECT, EJECT, EJECT! Don't hesitate to pull the D-ring located between your knees as soon as you hear that warning or you'll be flying a crippled jet aircraft to the ground all by yourself!" Actually, this wasn't entirely true as the instructor pilot would likely initiate automatic ejection sequence before we could react, and before we knew what was happening the canopy would be gone and we would be reaching for the sky with a rocket flaming out under our rear-ends. It was explained that the passenger in back (us) would be ejected first so that the pilot could eject safely without frying the rear-seater with the rocket charge on his seat. This is similar to most US ejection systems for tandem seating arrangements, and the protocol works much the same way. Only if the pilot in command were disabled would we be expected to initiate manual ejection for escape.

The Draken cockpit is, by the way, substantially co-
zier than the larger, more spacious cockpits of US
fighters. Of course, the Draken is somewhat smaller
in overall dimensions than comparable air defense
aircraft in the US, but it is still a considerably potent
adversary in air combat. The Draken ejection seat
is also slightly reclined in the same manner as the
General Dynamics F16's ACES II seat, a fact which
was surprising since the use of a reclining seat to
lessen the effects of G on aircrew in aerial combat
maneuvers (ACM) is a relatively recent development. The Draken's seat design precedes the
Falcon's by some 35 years!

After concluding the escape drills and egress system instruction, we were sent to the personal
equipment section and were fitted with the necessary gear for our upcoming flight on the next day:
helmet, oxygen mask, survival and life vest, anti-G
chaps, and other accessories required by the well-
turned-out aircrewman. Following this, orientation to
the actual Draken two-seater aircraft we were assigned to was carried out, in the hanger area.
Again, the Draken cockpit's relatively small size
was readily apparent as we squeezed down into the
SAAB aft ejection seats, being instructed in connections, fittings and so forth.

Ch. 11. RULE ONE FOR JOCKS...DON'T TALK SHIT:

With the final briefing over with, we doffed the personal equipment and were taken to the nearby Wing auditorium, where I was scheduled to deliver a prepared talk on the Convair F106A Delta Dart that is so similar to the SAAB Draken.

I had been told that my audience would consist of aircrew, ground support personnel, and life support people serving with the Wing, as well as pilots, air cadet students, and headquarters staff. The total number expected was unknown, but when I arrived I found about 150 people waiting to hear this Yank blather on about one of the lesser-known US supersonic Century Series fighters. Unfortunately, the impending Finnish National Holidays and midsummer celebrations that were about to take place had resulted in a lot of personnel taking off for early leave, but this was not necessarily a disappointment. Those present were easily identifiable--at least as far as flying personnel went, for pilots seem to uniformly affect a sort of cocky "What makes you think you can tell me anything new?" attitude (see the US movie TOP GUN for an example of this shit hot jock persona). The non-flying personnel also stood out as more attentive, less casual and somewhat more serious listeners, while the air cadets were the obviously animated onlookers and appeared ready to literally drink in anything at all having to do with the glamour of military flying-- even if it meant having to listen to a boring American visitor who wasn't even a rated pilot. The senior headquarters staff were also easy to spot, dressed in Class A blues, and more sober, older appearing--probably desk-flying members of the audience who now pushed pencils and wished they were still on active flying status.

I had prepared a fairly formal, somewhat technical presentation but found to my discomfort that my audience was substantially less formal than I had anticipated, and more interested in subjective experience than theoretical, historical background. With this in mind, and armed with a score of overhead transparencies, I tried to alter the nature of the presentation. It was a spotty go at best, and I could see some of the pilots evidencing boredom and not trying to hide it very well. I could only hope that some of those present would appreciate the fairly comprehensive study I gave them of US developed, delta-winged Cold War air defense fighters which formed the primary Cold War era front line inventory.

X Introduced me in Finnish, explaining that although I was not a rated pilot, I had served in SAC during the Vietnam War and had flown occasionally as unassigned aircrew in B52 bombers (BUFFs--Big Ugly Fat Fuckers, as we fondly knew them). That caught the interest of the audience, since Finland's young pilots have never had the opportunity to experience a real shooting war--every pilot's dream of fame and 'Right Stuff' glory. Then, after finishing up in his native language, X turned to me and said (in English): "...and I hope you will remember that all-important Rule Number One!" Picking up my prearranged cue, I faced the gathered listeners and remarked, *"Yes, X, it would never do to forget that all-important Rule Number One!"* I hoped that this would leave at least a few of the bored young fighter jocks curious as I began the speech.

About 45 minutes later and 20 overhead transparencies gone through, I brought the speech home with my concluding remarks. The mike was then opened up for questions, and I was hoping that someone would remember to ask what in hell 'Rule Number One' was. Since there were few questions--only one or two about the new stealth technology, which I was completely unable to deal with at any length--I took the ball back and asked, *"I suppose some of you are wondering what exactly that all-important Rule Number One is, eh?"* Actually, whether you are speaking to a group of pilots or flying hot military jets, it always pays to remember Rule Number One.... Rule Number One is *Ala puhuhu pasca!"* (Finnish for 'Don't talk shit'.) This indeed cracked a few otherwise serious or bored faces in the audience, since "Ala puhu pasca!" translates in English to "Don't talk shit!" Well, it was worth the cheap shot it amounted to, but for the most part the pilots remained largely laconic behind their shades. I had to remind myself that this disinterested affect is simply a 'fighter pilot thing'; it's merely part of the act.

Mercifully, the speech was over and done with. It turned out that not just the Wing's pilots, but the whole Wing's personnel were far more interested in the latest developments in stealth technology than in a not very well-known US military air defense fighter of the 60s and 70s. Several questions were

asked about this subject, and I had to admit igno-
rance of most of the specifics since that is not a
topic I am familiar enough with to speak extempora-
neously on. A few other questions were asked
about the US Air Force experience in the Vietnam-
ese war.

Several weeks before my visit I had taken a phone
call from the Wing Commander who asked if I could
come deliver an additional talk on this subject, but I
had to explain that all of my reference materials
were in the United States, and that I could not hope
to come up with anything of this complex nature on
such short notice, while in the Kingdom. I was
amazed to think they thought so much of me that I
could simply whip together an hour-long presentation on stealth technology. What was clear to me
when I had time to consider the experience of giving the speech afterwards was that the two hot
topics among the Finnish Air Force personnel were:
1) stealth technology, and 2) the Vietnam air war.

Finally, questions ended and I was surprised when
the Deputy Commander of the Satakunta Air Wing
presented me with a nicely framed black & white
framed photograph of two of the squadron's J-35
Draken fighters over the city of Tampere at sunset.
This was a token of appreciation in view of the fact
that I was speaking on the day of my 49th birthday--
June 19th--and it was a pleasing, unexpected me-
mento of my visit with the Central Finland Regional
Air Defense Center's Satakunta Air Wing. I managed to bring it back to the Kingdom with me intact,
despite the difficulty of trying to protect the framed

glass from breakage in the airliner's cramped luggage bin.

Ch. 12. HUEVOS RACHEROS A LA FINN:

By this time, it was late in the afternoon, and we loaded up the cramped Toyota once again for the short drive to the Finnish Defense Research Centre. The Draken flight was scheduled for the next day so we had some time to relax that evening with the research center's director. Dr. Z. met us after our arrival and took us to a country accommodation, sited beside a lake, that provided lodging and a recreation program for blind persons. The operator of the center was a former colleague of Dr. Z's, and everything from swimming to fishing and hiking was provided for sight-disadvantaged individuals under the supervision of trained staff. The concept is very Finnish, and the atmosphere of the resort was somewhere between a Japanese Ryokan and a Canadian wilderness hostel. Our stay at the place was quite pleasant, located as it was directly on a lake and surrounded by groves of birch trees. As might be expected, at the water's edge a quaint sauna was located, and situated so that one could step out the door and dive right into the lake.

After settling in to our rooms, Dr. Z. took X and I out for dinner. He asked us whether we wanted excellent atmosphere or excellent food. We opted for the latter and this turned out to be a Spanish restaurant named Salud!, which we were told had the reputation of having the most well-prepared food in all of Tampere. Dr. Z. was quite correct, and Salud! was a wonderful surprise, featuring a wide-ranging menu of Spanish specialties and a substantial wine-list. The dinner and conversation were a perfect

way to end a day such as we had experienced, and
Dr. Z. impressed me with his down-to-earth candor.
I enjoyed the meal even more due to the fact that I
hadn't had anything remotely resembling Spanish-
style food since leaving California a year before.

We arrived back at the resort well-sated and I began to appreciate what a uniquely intelligent and
congenial person our host was. Shortly after our return, we had another sauna. This time with several
of Dr. Z.'s colleagues from the Defense Research
Centre. Clustered around the stone hearth, the heat
and steam began to increase and in no time the
thermometer was hovering around 105 degrees. I
had resolved not to flinch, and was determined to
demonstrate that I was as able to handle the heat
as any Finnish sauna devotee. There were beer
and the usual snacks on hand and this time we un-
derwent 3 cycles of about 15 minutes each,
interspersed with quick trips out to the lake where
the chill lake water threatened to perform another
cryosurgical alteration of a certain part of me. Actually, it wasn't as bad as I had anticipated, as I was
this time a bit better prepared for the experience. I
managed to dive in, like the others, and swan two
laps from the dock to a buoy and back. Aside from
a purplish cast to my skin, I survived each of these
dips in fairly good order. The conversation with Dr.
Z were very interesting since he has maintained a
life-long interest in aviation and has a son who flies
Drakens with the Satakunta Wing. Dr. Z. is a very
down-to-earth person, despite his august creden-
tials as chief of the Defense Research Centre, and
my friend X later remarked that he is renowned for
always treating others as if they were his equals, no

matter what the context or situation. His humility and great knowledge of things impressed me greatly and we sat about in the steam, drinking good Finnish beer while the mosquito squadrons droned off the lake and into the air around us. As expected, Dr. Z.'s English was excellent, and he had quite a refreshing sense of humor as well. Whoever thinks the Finns, as a people, are morose and reserved has obviously never encountered the Finns I had met so far on this trip!

The next morning, we met Dr. Z. at the Defense Research Centre for a special tour of that facility. The Finnish Defense Research Centre is responsible for all the military and defense-related projects carried out within the aegis of the Finnish Armed Forces. Of especial interest to X and I were the laboratories in which their chemical and biological protection studies were performed, and it was fascinating to view the hermetically sealed containment areas wherein deadly toxins and virulent biological organisms were being studied for the development of defensive measures. Here were real-live counterparts of the bogus biological lab movie-sets featured in the movie OUTBREAK! and it was quite sobering to be mere inches from such deadly substances as Anthrax and Ebola.

Dr. Z. presented us with a slide and overhead projection lecture detailing the mission and scope of the defense center's operations, after a break for some excellent Finnish coffee and pastries; then we were taken to the center's cafeteria and were treated to a typical Finnish dinner, such as the employees enjoyed. The cafeteria is situated in what used to be part of an old copper mine complex that originally occupied the site upon which the Defense Research Centre has been developed. Next to the cafeteria building is a very deep artificial lake--a remnant of the former pit copper mining operation. We were told the lake was still too acidic to permit it to be stocked with fish but that in another 10 years such an enhancement might be possible.

The dinner we were treated to was substantial and sumptuous, a good example of how seriously the Finns take their dining, even in an institution. There was a unique Finnish beverage served with the meal which was dark and made from hops and grain. It is actually a sweetish sort of beer without the alcohol. Unusual, but very refreshing. Once again, after thanking Dr. Z. for his excellent hospitality, X and I waddled with full bellies out to the small Toyota (which seemed to be even smaller after all that good food!). Security clearances turned in at the main gate to the center, we drove out and headed back to the Satakunta Air Wing facility, which shares the Tampere Airport runways with civilian air traffic. This was to be the highlight of our trip--the main event: a flight in a Draken fighter!

Ch. 13. MOVE OVER, CHUCK YEAGER &
TOM CRUISE:

The Satakunta Air Wing life support people took X
and I in tow shortly after arrival, and we headed for
one of the hangers accompanied by the base Deputy Commander (who is rated for Drakens). One of
the Commander's adjutants gave us a last briefing
on egress procedures and then went through a run-
down on the flight profile which we would be
engaging in, once in the air. Then we visited the life
support shop where we were again fitted with our
personal equipment, and a staff car drove us out to
the ramp where two SK-35C two-seat Draken trainers stood, side by side, awaiting us in their dark,
forest-green camouflage (the Satakunta Air Wing
facilities are on the opposite side of the Tampere
Airport's main runways, and military aircraft must
taxi a short distance out to the adjoining taxiways
for take-off). No photographs were permitted, of
course, due to security concerns; this was a pity,
since it would have been nice to have some photo-
graphic souvenirs of the flights.

The Drakens are impressive machines, despite being built rather lower to the ground than comparable
American fighters. Still, they give the impression of
being a bit more toy-like than the Convair F106A
Delta Dart we used to fly. Any fallacious assump-
tions of this sort quickly dissipate, however, as soon
as the throttle quadrant of the SAAB engine is
pushed forward into full reheat position and the

characteristic, shattering banshee howl of the Draken engine bursts forth to announce that take-off is imminent.

First, a preliminary walk-around inspection of each of the two Drakens was completed. Then, mounting the cockpit ladders, X and I were literally shoe-horned into the cramped crew-spaces of the machines, each of us in a separate aircraft, along with the instructor pilot who would fly the mission. A last-minute check, connections to life support all engaged and then the canopies were lowered and sealed. It was finally time to GET REAL!

The preflight checklist was run through, engines powered up and we rolled out onto the taxiways to the main runway where final preflight items were checked off. At last clearance was received from Tampere tower ground control, and engine RPMs were increased as the turbines spooled up with the brakes kept firmly on. You could feel the powerful SAAB engine straining against the brakes, trying to break free until the throttle was pushed full into the afterburner detent...suddenly, WHAM! We were slammed back into our ejection seats as the Drakens rolled down the runway, finally turned loose. Even through the sound deadening effect of our helmet headsets we could hear the scream of these powerful engines. The takeoff-roll quickly increased and the full force of the Draken engine became apparent as speed built up until V1 was reached, then V2. Finally, the nose lifted to an angle of attack of about 15 degrees as the planes broke free of the ground effect and slashed up into the grey Finnish sky. The noise to bystanders is quite loud and one knows, even without seeing an aircraft, that a Draken is in the immediate vicinity from all the bone-shaking sound the Draken engine generates on full reheat.

Ch 14. FAST COMPANY & LABORED BREATHING:

Pullout was smooth, then the snick of wheels up and locked and we were making speed out of the pattern and reaching for altitude. The mission we were flying was a mock air intercept to the north-- the precise details of the flight would be too complex and doubtless boring to recount here, but suffice to say that an intercept altitude of about 40,000 feet was reached as we were vectored to the IP (Initial Point) by ground control at slightly over Mach 1. Contact, given the distances involved in Finnish terrain, was not far from being established quickly. I strained for a visual contact from my seat; encumbered by all my flight gear and coping with the pressure demand breathing of the mask, I still managed to get some excellent views of the north Finland countryside. The lakes that the Finnish map shows are all over the country are really all there, like so many thousands of small mirrors reflecting sunlight back from the ground. I could only imagine what the sight must be in the winter, when all are sheets of solid ice.

Breathing 100% oxygen at that altitude via pressure is a task that takes some getting used to, for the technique is the exact reverse of normal breathing at sea-level. Oxygen flows under pressure in through the mask until one exhales forcefully. This stops the flow until the exhalation is stopped and pressurised oxygen begins to flow in once more. Experienced over a period of time, it can be a bit fatiguing and some training in use of pressure breathing is usually required. With visual impairment and cerebral dysfunction, a concern in flying at high altitudes, normal practice for military aviation is to maintain 100% oxygen at all times while flying at night, and pressurised breathing of 100% oxygen is maintained during all flights above 20,000 feet.

It wasn't long before the relatively short, fast flight resulted in an interception with the simulated Finnish air space penetration--in this case a Hawk trainer playing "bad guy." Quickly a weapons lock was established and AIM type missiles were dry fired. Immediately thereafter we broke off contact, the Hawk's electronic hit receiving equipment confirming a probably kill, and we vectored back to Tampere and home base at a rather leisurely Mach 0.85.

I had some moments to examine the cockpit more in detail then, and while I was lost in thought the pilot of my Draken come on the interphone and asked me if I wanted to take the stick? My call sign at that moment could have been *Sweaty Palms*, for the excitement of taking control of a plane of this size and performance was unexpected--I had thought we would simply be having a guided tour with our chauffeur! Replying in the affirmative however, I placed my hand on the control stick grip, taking care not to accidentally flip any switches, and waited for the signal that I had the craft. For about 2 minutes afterwards I had the reins of this beautiful green 40-year old beast in my hand and it felt absolutely fantastic! Of course, I knew better than to do anything more than hold it on a straight and level course, but it was still a big thrill. I've been up in the back seats of other military jets before but have rarely had the courtesy of actually taking the stick offered. The Instructor Pilot who was flying our plane was undoubtedly closely shadowing my movements, his hand loosely grasping the stick in the front office to be ready to take control if anything untoward happened--I know it's a sham, and he knows it's a sham, but hey!...I'll settle for that fantasy any day! Me and Tom Cruise, up there on wings of flame at the age of 49! Looking off the port wing I could see X in the back seat of his SK-35C Draken, holding station with us as we neared home. I could imagine there was as big a grin behind the face-visor of his helmet as I had behind mine.

Ch. 15. BACK TO EARTH & REALITY:

I could have gladly answered the Celestial Trumpet Call at that moment with no regrets, but the flight continued, of course. After a few minutes of extremely gentle banking and a slight nose-down maneuver--it was so slight you would have thought the pilot hiccupped--I relinquished control to my pilot once more and we shortly thereafter assumed our descent vector for final approach to Tampere, orbiting the field for a few circuits while a commercial airliner took off. Then it was roll out and base leg before dropping like a rock over the field's outer marker The Draken's engine screamed like the thunder of the Norse Gods, now that we were lower and slower, and it was easier to hear the cavernous wail of its internal guts howling like a banshee. Finally, we were a few seconds from touchdown, noise in a characteristically high attitude for delta winged aircraft, and the rise and fall of the engine's wail changed with each alteration of the engine's throttle detent as the pilot sought that magic combination of power, angle of attack, speed and flaperon settings to land us precisely on our main gear. A delta doesn't have conventional control surfaces; instead of ailerons, elevators, and flaps a delta used flaperons, which combine the several functions. Landing a big delta is no small matter, although to witness an accomplished pilot do it (as we did several times that day, after the flight) from the vantage of the nearby ground is like watching a modern-day Toscanini conduct Mahler--pure brilliant art! The nose of a delta has to be kept at a fairly high angle of attack, both in take-off and in landing, with appreciable airspeed in order to generate the desired lift; once the main gear kiss the runway after floating on the ground effect for a second the nose is kept high to help use aerodynamic braking forces to kill airspeed and maintained in this angle of attack until the airspeed falls away and the nose gently falls onto the runway of its own accord. The drag chute on the Draken is especially helpful as it enables the aircraft to land on very short runways, or even on highways used as wartime emergency strips. Behind us X's Draken executed a perfect landing not long after our own craft had touched down and they joined us for a picture-perfect promenade down the tarmac back to the hangers.

By the time we finally came to a stop, engine cut and canopy released, it was just starting to get a bit misty high overhead. We had had a great flight, perfect weather (just got back ahead of a thunderstorm that was rolling in) and a superb introduction to this classic Swedish designed and Finnish made air defense interceptor—a near counterpart to America's own Convair F106A Delta Dart. Disconnecting my gear from the aircraft's life support system, I eased myself out of the cramped Draken cockpit with the help of several grinning ground crewmen and clambered down the crew ladder ahead of the pilot, who was running down a final post-flight checklist.

To say I was stoked would be understating the feeling--I felt like an old Berkeley pot-head after three sticks of Manzanillo Blue. So strong was the "righteous brother" feeling that I hated to take off my gear after the flight, wanting to prolong the mood just a bit longer! This was, aside from a flight in an F106, the nearest I had ever come to joining the righteous brotherhood. But, all things must end sooner or later and we climbed into the transport vehicle for a ride back to life support where we turned in our personal equipment and joined up with the base's Deputy Commander for a few cups of strong coffee and some post-flight exuberance. Our pilots joined us after a few minutes, and I found out that mine was only 25 years old. I instantly felt like something of a fossil when I considered how righteous his stuff was at almost exactly half my own age, but reminded myself that the job of flying today's hot aircraft is rightfully the preserve of young guys in their 20s with the sharply honed reflexes that such complex aircraft and demanding flying requires. In fact, the younger they are the better--assuming a certain quotient of resident maturity--since new, state of the art designs require youthful reflexes and alertness. Just watch any teenager playing video games to appreciate this essence requirement that confers a decided tactical advantage in negotiating the world of razor-sharp leading-edge performance envelopes.

After some stimulating "hanger flying" and male bonding rituals with the base DC and our pilots, we made ready to depart, thanking everyone once again for giving us the unique and long-to-be-remembered experience of being treated to a flight in one of the world's most interesting contemporary delta-winged jet fighters. Soon we were ready, gear loaded. With one last fond look at the two green dragons we had flown in, we were off once again--this time headed for the Finnish School of NBC Defense, which is located in Keuruu at the headquarters of the Central Finland Regiment. A whole new set of experiences were soon to follow, and undoubtedly a few more saunas to go along with them! I thought it likely that I would end up resembling one of our famous California Raisins before this trip was over--or at least a wrinkled prune!

Ch. 16. FINNISH SCHOOL OF NBC DE-FENSE:

We arrived at Regimental Headquarters just outside of the town of Keuruu in central Finland a bit later, having linked up at the air base with another colleague of X's--a young Finnish doctoral candidate and author/historian who recently wrote a definitive history of the Finnish's Defense Forces' chemical warfare service. I rode with him in his pleasantly dilapidated old Saab model 96 sedan. He was writing his thesis on a theory centered on the idea that war threats dictate social response, thereby profoundly affecting changes experienced by civilisation, and I welcomed the opportunity to discuss these things with him as we rolled through the beautiful countryside is his cranky old red Saab. "J" is quite a sharp fellow and in addition to having some fun sharing jokes about his old car, we got down to some serious interchanges on his thesis. Necessarily complicated and too long to set down briefly, he theorises that a specific set of social changes were motivated by three specifically monumental threat posed to civilisation in the past century: two of these threats were chemical and nuclear war, and the third eludes me. At any rate, we spent the better part of our trip in frequently animated conversation and before long we were entering Keuruu, a delightfully pastoral, semi-rural community whose name in Finnish means "Caribou." I had earlier received a copy of J's book; detailing 50 years of Finnish chemical warfare service history, from 1944 through 1994, it is about 240 pages in length and illustrated with some interesting photo plates.

Pulling up to the Central Finland Regiment's training facilities, we were met by Colonel T., the Commandant of the NBC School. I had met him in Stockholm and periodically throughout the conference there, but this was the first time I had had a chance to get to know him a bit more. We joined his adjutant, a young First Lieutenant who had also been in Stockholm (and a friend of X's), and started a tour of the NBC School after dropping our things off at the Bachelor Officers' Quarters. Finland has a conscript program, wherein all young Finnish males spend a certain number of months in mandatory national service. X had formerly been a chemical warfare service sergeant in his conscript days and accordingly, he knew everyone there at the Regimental Headquarters quite well. Formerly a central figure in developing the historical concerns and museum maintained there at the NBC School, X had maintained his associations and contacts. It would possibly be of interest, here, to explain a bit about just how the Finnish military conscription service works.

In Finland, there is a mandatory 11-month conscription for all young men reaching their 18th or 19th birthday. After initial induction, they are given both basic and specialised training courses. When their 11-month mandatory service is completed they go on active reserve status for a further period of time and are subject to immediate call-up in the event of a national emergency. Most young Finns hate the national service requirement, understandably, but comply with it. It is during this 11-month period of initial required service that selections are made for

officer candidates and from this common start some
are sent off to military academy, while others are
assigned to different assignments leading to permanent military careers. Finland has a proud and long
history of military traditions, but given contemporary
social enlightenment and the world-wide rebellious-
ness of youth, it is perhaps understandable that
most young conscripts find national service distasteful nonetheless. The officer Corps are more
profession oriented and have a far higher esprit de
corps; conscript attitudes vary towards their military
duties, obviously, but disinterest predominates:
"Let's just get it over with."

I was a bit surprised how informally the nominal military courtesies are rendered (in my short period of
observation at Keuruu) by the conscripts. Salutes
are still given and returned but there is an evident
and studies casualness in the exchange. The basic
conscriptee attitude changes quickly enough, I was
told, after exposure to the drill sergeants in basic
training. Not that much different from our own
American system after all, apparently.

Colonel T. quickly demonstrated his genuine friend-
liness and hospitality, and of course I had already
had some introduction to Lt. J. (who had been in
charge of the new Finnish M-95 chemical respirator
Army field trials) in Stockholm. Quite quickly we all
became seemingly good friends and after some
briefings in the NBC School pertaining to mission,
scope of activity, etc., we ended our tour of the
school with a visit to the chemical warfare museum
displays that X had originally been responsible for
setting up. Gathering outside for a few photographs

in the hazy afternoon sun, we then got into a staff car and took a short ride to the nearby lake, where a program of aircrew water-survival was in progress.

Ch. 17. PARACHUTES AND RUBBER DUCKIES:

Satakunta Air Wing aircrew water survival training takes place at a site along the shore of the lake about a km from the main base itself. This consists of fitting up about 12 Finnish Draken & *Mig-21F bis* pilots in full survival gear--personal equipment required for flights over water included--and then using a specially adapted paragliding chute system and power boat to tow them up to an altitude of about 1000 feet over the lake. This is not unlike the paragliding that tourists to Mexico's beaches can experience for a price except for one large difference: when the pilot reaches 1000 feet of altitude the chute is released from the tow-cable and the descent to the lake below begins, laden with a considerable load of heavy equipment. The idea is to teach aircrew to quickly be able to deploy water-survival kits, pulling the lanyard that releases the life raft and landing successfully in the water without becoming ensnarled in the parachute or its risers. Once in the water, the chute harness's Capewells (chute attachment connectors) are released and you heave yourself up and over the side of a smallish (6 feet long) personal life raft, setting off a smoke signal to help air-rescue spot you. A Finnish Air Force MI-8 Hind (Russian made) chopper then sweeps over the lake to make a winch-rescue pick-up of the downed pilot, and the exercise is completed.

X and I were taken out to the anchored pontoon craft, with Lt. J and Colonel T., where the survival training was taking place in one of the regimental motor boats. There we met Major R. of the Finnish Air Force, who was in charge of the exercise. After observing the training for a while, Major R. offered to let X and I go up. This promised to be quite an interesting undertaking, and an opportunity to prove that we could come down into the cold drink and emerge successfully without swallowing half the lake or turning blue in the process. X and I accepted the offer and were suited up in brightly colored water exposure suits worn by Finnish pilots on over-water missions (in Finland that is pretty much most of the time, as in addition to its Bothnian Gulf shoreline, there are thousands of lakes scattered all over the country). Then full flight gear followed--helmets, oxygen masks, life vest, survival equipment, harness, and finally, the yellow colored training survival kit itself. On the Draken, Hawk and Hornet aircraft these are carried under the seat cushion of the ejection seats; a similar arrangement is configured for kits used with the *Mig-21F bis* aircraft (Russian system).

X and I watched the aircrew going up before us with interest and then it was finally our turn. When it was my shot, the bright yellow and orange paragliding canopy was attached to the harness Capewells and I stood poised on the edge of the pontoon. Behind me, several others held the chute's nylon in a semi-open display so as to catch the wind quickly when the tow-boat began the tow.

The tow cable was attached to a special quick-release on my harness, and then on the given signal the powerboat throttled forward, much like a waterskiing ride begins. The lines snapped taut, although there was a minor moment of slack in the tow just before it took my full weight and I got a quick dunking up to my knees in the lake before the chute started to carry me aloft. After getting my feet wet, we were on our way up to 1000 feet and I was soon contemplating how cold and deep blue the lake looked from this height.

Moments later came the release, and with a sharp metallic snap I was on my way down to reacquaint myself with that frigid mass of water. The chute was still wet from its previous use and was therefore a bit heavier that it would normally be; this combined with the heavy weight of the survival kit meant the trip down was somewhat faster than I had expected. I remembered to drop the survival kit's lanyard about half way down, allowing it to snake out to the end of a 20-foot nylon line below me, and braced for the plunge. The water contact switch on the life raft would cause it to self-inflate, and all I had to do was swim sputtering up from beneath the lake's surface, release my chute harness Capewells and disconnect one of the oxygen mask's bayonets so that I could breathe. Easy enough to say; a bit harder to do in sequence, but amazingly, the push of adrenal expediency facilitates the drill. The life vest inflated quickly enough, but the cold of the lake's water could be felt, despite the anti-exposure suit's insulation. I wondered what the Gulf of Bothnia would feel like after an hour in the drink there, remembering how it had felt in the relatively warm shallows along its shoreline in Vaasa--without an exposure suit!

The next moment was easy, if you disallow the somewhat less than perfect immersion suit quality. I grabbed the life raft line and started to try to roll over the edge of it in the demonstrated manner, finding it a bit harder to accomplish than it had appeared. Finally, after two or three attempts, I managed to settle into the snug raft and grabbed a smoke signal from my survival vest, setting off the bright orange plume to drift lazily skyward. As the nearby paragliding chute canopy was gathered up by the powerboat crew to be taken back for use by the next trainee, I scanned the sky for the big black Hind chopper that would come pick me up.

It was there quickly enough, having been hovering just above the shore line, and a winch cable was lowered which I snapped onto my harness for a dizzying lift up to the gaping hatch of the big machine. After stumbling on board, and strapping in to a web seat, I glanced around at the crew. All were grinning under their helmets--I suppose thinking how unusual a break from the ordinary it was to be ferrying a visiting foreigner instead of the usual squadron aircrew. I grinned back and got a thumbs-up from the crew chief as we flew back to the pontoon's staging area where X, Lt. J., and Colonel T. waited. The massively built Russian MI-8 Hind is something else to experience from the inside. Noisy, bulky and huge are the only adequate words to describe it. I understand they are, however, relatively reliable when maintained by experienced mechanics, and the Finnish Defense Forces have used them for some time with success. They are a lot cheaper, naturally, than North American or European counterparts are to fly and maintain.

After X's jump was completed, we took our leave of the Major R. and the aircrew survival training sessions, getting into the regimental motor-boat for a trip around the lake before heading back. I was surprised to find us docking, after a bit, at a swank water-front resort with a large sun balcony and lake-front alfresco café. Colonel T. explained to X and I that we would be his guests for some good Finnish beer there, and the next hour was spent sitting about quaffing Quality III KOFF brew enjoying some good discussion on the survival training in the setting of the resort's scenic locale. In a ground level barbeque, the hotel staff were building a big birch-wood fire in the coals of which, J. explained, the restaurant's traditional entrée was buried and left to bake for several hours--something along the lines of a Hawaiian Luau. A bit later, feeling no pain and considerably relaxed by the good beer--the cold of the lake water forgotten--all of us piled back in the regimental motor-launch for the return trip back to the facility.

Casting off from shore, we poled out a bit and the Finnish conscript operating the launch tried to start the small outboard engine; it was balky and wouldn't start, the poor conscript nearly exhausting himself trying to coax it to life. Alternating turns on the motor's rope-pull, each of us gave it our best effort, despite the effects of the beer. This continued for about 15 minutes and accomplished nothing except that each attempt to start the engine had pushed us further and further into the lake. Finally, the realisation settled into all of us that the engine was not going to start, but we were several hundred meters from shore, about a half mile away from the survival training pontoon, and none of us relished the thought of having to dive into the lake and attempt to pull the boat to shore.

Fortunately, it was a sunny afternoon, we were all pretty happy to just sit there for a while, what with the beer and all, and eventually another launch from the regiment making courier rounds on the lake noticed us and we were able to get a tow back to the regimental facility. Colonel T. took it all in the best of humor, even though he must have been a bit embarrassed to have his boat become disabled while taking us on our tour. He made a few self-deprecating jokes about how this was not an operational motor but rather just a training one.

"Hmmmm, Finnish motor Pirkkala!," he said with a forced grin, ironically alluding to the fact that the company that made the outboard motor was soon going to be making the new Finnish-license version of the McDonnell-Douglas FA-18 Hornet for the Finnish Air Force--the official Draken replacement just starting to be manufactured. Better a failed outboard engine than a high performance supersonic jet turbine engine, we all agreed with some humor. Shortly thereafter, the launch docked and we all had some more beer in the Officers' Club, before being shown to our quarters for the night's lodging. What a day it had been, and what a great introduction to the Finnish people! I was loving it!

Ch. 18. ONCE MORE, WITH FEELING:

Later that evening we were treated to yet another sauna, this time in the Officers' Club with Colonel T., Lt. J., X and a few others. There was no lake nearby to swim in, since it was a bit removed from the site, but we steamed at 100 degrees anyway and came out periodically for snacks and more beer. Immediately afterwards there was to be a dinner in the mess. X approached me and asked if I would consider giving my Satakunta Air Wing speech on the Convair F106 interceptor to the regimental personnel and a detachment of the pilots and air cadets who were attending the water survival training. This was completely unexpected and I had already had a fair quantity of Quality III KOFF beer by this time, courtesy of Colonel T. However, the beer had worked its "Irish Courage Effect" and after a quick self-assessment of my coherency, I decided 'why the hell not?' We brought out the overhead projector and as the group finished its meal and settled back into some more beer, I launched again into a somewhat sharpened-up version of the talk I have given at the airbase--this time better prepared for the casual nature of the gathering. Amazingly, the beer actually helped me, rather than having the opposite effect, and I was soon into my Chuck Yeager/Tom Cruise fighter pilot synthesis--a transition by the realisation that the Draken and MiG pilots present were all in their 20s while the air cadets were in their teens.

Accordingly, things went far better this time, my confidence visibly supported by the ETOH (shameful to admit), and I brought the whole presentation off with aplomb and almost a certain amount of finesse. The audience gave ready approval of the talk this time--none of that fighter jock posing. Even the Draken pilots were more responsive with the Tom Cruise "cool" act forgotten as I got into the meat of the historical development of the Convair F106 aircraft and the American Air Defense strategy of the Cold War Era. Once again X and I played the Rule Number One routine--this time with gratifying results. It produced a roar of approval and laughter from everyone present. This response was undoubtedly amplified by the quantities of beer being consumed after a rigorous day in water survival training on the lake, but it highlights the difference between sober pilots contemplating a serious subject given seriously, and happily "mood-adjusted" pilots enjoying the same thing given by an equally "mood-adjusted" colleague in a casual setting. The evening was therefore a great personal success, and enjoyed by all of us.

The air cadets left the hall with a slight sheen in their eyes, doubtless produced by a combination of the beer and their heady romantic dreams of someday joining the ranks of their older righteous brothers; the Draken & MiG pilots (those who weren't flying the next day) stayed on for a bit more hanger flying at the table with us, and after another hour of so we all returned to our rooms at the O Club for some well-deserved sleep in the amazingly comfortable beds there (not like US Air Force BOQ, that's for sure!).

I slept like a baby that night, my last thoughts before bailing out of the conscious world wondering
how my wife was doing with X's wife, taking in the
many interesting sights that Finland has to offer.
Just prior to nodding off I mused briefly over the
"typical" Finnish personality. Everyone in Finland I
had had the initial appearance of being very serious
about even the slightest detail, but I had soon
learned that this was really only a façade produced
by Finnish society's proprietary etiquette. Under
that masque of polite detachment there was usually
a smile and a laugh lurking, just waiting to spring
forth. Many times, good fellowship and similar interests alone produced the desired icebreaker, but I
noticed that frequently enough good Finnish beer,
although expensive, was a useful inhibition-reduc-
tion agent, and so was the cherished ritual of the
sauna. There seems to be an inherent "shyness"
about the Finns--especially among men--and this
characteristic is often misread, so it would seem, by
non-Finns as being an air of disinterested aloof-
ness. How much farther from the truth one could
get, I couldn't imagine. By the time I was ready to
emplane for Riyadh at the end of our trip, I felt I had
made many genuinely sincere new friends and acquaintances; the Finland of my acquaintance is
truly an amazingly warm-hearted nation, and so
very different from Sweden.

Ch. 19. AVIATION MUSEUMS & FINNISH GIRLS:

Early the next morning X and I gathered up our things once again--my stock of clean clothes was beginning to run short after almost two weeks living out of suitcases--and again loaded up the car for our departure. A last brief tour of the civil township of Keuruu was given us by Colonel T. and Lt. J. in the regimental staff car, and the highlight of this was a stop to see the oldest wooden Finnish church in the nation. Designed and built by an uneducated, self-taught carpenter in the mid 1700's, the Keuruu church is a masterpiece of architecture in the rustic Scandinavian style. It was an amazing sight, looming tall and silhouetted in the mid-June sun of Finland's summer.

Once back at the base, once more, we received a call from Professor K. at the Research Center, suggesting that we stop by the interesting aviation museum in his native home-region near the city of Halle; this museum is close by the Finnish air base where all the secret Finnish flight testing is done, and Professor K. went on to say he would meet us there, since he was taking an early mid-summer holiday.

As we drove to Halle from Keuruu, X pulled out some cassette tapes and asked me if I like American rock & roll. When I replied that I did, I was amazed and a bit tickled to hear a collection of classic R&R from the late 60s and 70s, which X had selected and recorded himself. Garcia, Hendrix,

The Dead, Jefferson Airplane, BTO, Lynerd Skyn-
erd--all my favorites. I was having a great time--
couldn't have picked the pieces better myself. What
a guy X was turning out to be. He was fascinated
when I told him I had listened to many of these
groups live in San Francisco during the Haight-Ash-
bury days, but was visibly disappointed when I told
him I had missed out on Woodstock, due to its being so far away (Finland is a smaller country and
the difference in sizes is sometimes lost in the comparison). The Finns, of course, have a profound
liking for American pop music--especially jazz and
R&R. In fact, Professor K. had earlier confessed
during our sauna together that he played sax in a
Finnish jazz group. I had told him at that time that I
used to play Trombone and he said it was a shame
he hadn't known that or we could have gotten together in a session. Hah!

The aviation museum at Halle, home of the Finnish
airline Carhu and the original, indigenous Finnish
Valmet Aircraft Works, is something that has to be
seen to be believed. From the road, sitting under a
cover of trees, it gives the impression of being a
nondescript collection of large and small buildings.
That was my feeling when we pulled off the road after driving down from Keuruu. Professor K. was
already there, so we got out and were introduced to
a Finnish Air Force Major who had agreed to give
us a personal tour of the facility. The Major spoke
excellent English, as do most Finnish Air Force personnel (English is the international language of
flight, after all), and just before we entered the reception area Professor K. asked me, in the course
of some small talk, what I thought of Finnish

women. When I replied that I hadn't really had a chance to meet any, he told me with a smile that this was probably just as well since once I had met a few I wouldn't want to leave Finland!

As if to prove his point, there sitting behind the desk of the reception office for the Halle Aviation Museum was one of the most stunningly beautiful girls I have ever seen. With lovely long brown hair, a healthy tanned skin and the body of a gazelle, she was smiling with what had to be the most genuinely friendly interest I have seen on a woman of such beauty. And she must have been all of 18. This was Annika, who was a volunteer at the museum, and whose father was an officer at the nearby air base. Glancing away from pretty Annika, I looked over at Professor K. who was smiling himself quite broadly, as if to say "What did I tell you?"

The first building, which adjoined the reception office, was something of a disappointment as it contained nothing but copies of aviation manuals, books, and technical & maintenance references of all ages and periods. Thinking this was the whole show, I was a bit let down but kept this feeling to myself. It was, after all, a valuable repository for all sorts of priceless information regarding aircraft, even if almost all of it was in Finnish & Swedish.

We left this building and walked under the trees to the one next door: here was the real gold mine and treasure trove I had been hoping for! Row after row of artifacts awaited inspection, and among them a whole section dedicated to ejection seats from Finnish aircraft. These included two Martin-Baker

(English) Mark 3B seats (relatively early productions), a seat from a Russian Ilyushin IL-28 bomber, the seat and canopy from a Russian MiG-21F bis, and one from an early English Folland Gnat jet trainer. What a great find for an old life support specialist like myself!

There were lots of other interesting items nearby, including an extremely rare World War Two German Luftwaffe oxygen mask, made by Dräger, and including the original rubber hose and component parts. This mask was the precursor design inspiration for all US Air Force pressure-demand oxygen masks produced since the war and through the 60s. A great example of the influence not only of German aeronautical design but of the innovative value of German aerospace medical achievements produced before the end of that war. There must be fewer than a handful of these masks left anywhere in the whole world, since they were manufactured from native rubber and it is only a matter of time before those which still survive are left to dry up and rot away from ozone and ultraviolet light effects. I urged the Major showing us around that this mask be specially protected in a sealed container, so that it would remain preserved.; as it was being displayed, it was simply sitting on an open table top without any protection from the air or sunlight whatsoever.

The tour concluded with a visit to still a third, somewhat larger building that gave the appearance of having originally been a hanger. Outside it was parked a MiG-17 two-seat trainer, while within were six more well-preserved Finnish aircraft around which were tucked still more displays. We spent several hours altogether admiring the many interesting things to see in this somewhat casually organised but fascinating museum, Professor K. apparently just as happy seeing all these exhibits as X and I. Finally, however, we were reluctantly able to tear ourselves away from the aeronautical displays and thanked the Major for his assistance in seeing everything. Once in our cars, we drove up the nearby road to the top of a small plateau. This, Professor K. told us, was the edge of the secret air base where Finnish aeronautical flight testing is undertaken. We got out and stood at the cyclone fencing for a while, hoping to see some aircraft come in or take off. Not long after a Draken came swooping in low on base leg, did a very fast, low turn onto the glide slope and came in hot. It was obviously a pilot of exceptional skill in the plane's cockpit, judging from the way he rode this supersonic dragon in like a motorcycle in a tight turn.

Our appreciation was short-lived, however, since by that time the perimeter guards, armed with automatic weapons and accompanied by guard dogs, had spotted us and arrived by bicycle to tell us to clear the area. Even though we were on the other side of the security fence, they made it clear that we were not even allowed to look through the fence. Professor K. showed them his government identification as director of the national defense research labs but this produced no response from the young, earnest guards who looked a bit nervous, weapons unshouldered. I didn't realise until Professor K. told me later that they were under orders to keep people away at any cost. Such, apparently, is a decidedly non-casual attitude towards security in otherwise friendly Finland. Those boys were indeed serious! Getting back into the cars, we drove off, back down the road and out to Professor K's beautiful country home on a nearby lake.

The cottage, if a large, multi-bed roomed wood-log built structure built in the traditional Finnish custom can be called a cottage, was beautifully situated with a view of the lake and its own dock. Professor K. showed us around, pointed out his own smoke sauna said that next time I came through we would be his guests in it. With that, X and I said our good-byes and headed back across the Finnish forests to X's wife's parents' house, just outside the city of Lahti, where we had arranged earlier to meet our wives.

Ch 20. MOSQUITOES AND MIDSUMMER:

That evening and night was spent with these good people, who spoke no English but were very cordial and hospitable. Despite the language barrier, we all got along quite well and met the other relatives who were arriving to spend the traditional Finnish Mid-Summer Holiday with them. There was good food on the outdoor grill when we arrived and a lot of that excellent and strong Finnish coffee, as well.

Irene had had a great time seeing Finland with X's wife, but she confessed to me that having to speak good English clearly and carefully all the time was finally a bit exhausting for her. I reminded her that it was probably as difficult for X's wife, speaking in a non-native language as she was, and this was a consciousness raising moment for both of us. Between us, we speak 5 different languages with more or less fluency, but nothing even faintly similar to the Finno-Ugric tongue whose most near linguistic relative is probably Estonian. Finnish, as a written and spoken language, has virtually nothing in common with the other Scandinavian languages, contrary to popular American misperceptions and Swedish political domination of Finland up until recent times.

The cabin was sited near a local lake so the mosquitoes were particularly thick. My wife was their especial target, seemingly, as they always zero in on her as a tastier morsel than my own wizened hide. Despite this fact, after dinner, we all walked to

the lake, unhitched the family skiff and I demonstrated by old Boy Scout small craft handling skills
to them by rowing us around the lake's inlets. The
skills and techniques were still there in my hands,
as I successfully rediscovered all the strokes in the
course of the next hour. There were several small
islands in the lake which we visited and evidence of
a number of small vacation cottages dotted around
the lake's perimeter: everyone was there for the
mid-summer holiday. I found that by maintaining a
fair rate of speed we could keep some of the mosquito squadrons at bay, and the tour was conducted
at a fairly fast pace. Despite the pests, I enjoyed the
chance to keep my muscles in tone since I hadn't
been doing any exercise since I left Riyadh, weeks
before. The others were all too happy to let me provide the muscle work. I couldn't help but think about
how near idyllic Finland can be at such moments,
and wondered what it would be like to be a citizen
and be able to live here as a resident.

I mentioned this to X as the sun was setting, leaving a beautiful golden glow in the sky; after a
moment, he replied that I might not feel as elated if
I had to cope with the minus 40-degree winters, as
well. To this I demurred, protesting my preference
for truly cold-ass winters such as I had experienced
in North Dakota, during my active duty with the US
Air Force. X found that a bit hard to believe, as their
preference runs towards the sun, it being such a
rare and precious commodity in Finland.

All over the lake, as we headed back to the cottage,
Finns were celebrating Mid-Summer Festival. Big
bonfires were being stacked up on the beaches and

the jovial, enthusiastic excitement generated was infectious. As a result, we hardly noticed the mosquitoes and the Finns themselves seem almost unaware of the them, so used to them have they become. I think if I lived in a natively beautiful a land as Finland is I'd be willing to endure a few flying pests in the bargain. Oddly enough, as an aviation-minded person, I found myself musing that even though they are a nuisance, they do have the natural ability to fly--unlike us poor, ground-bound creatures who have to settle for some decidedly unnatural and artificial techniques to defy gravity for a brief while.

By 10 PM I was ready for bed after a full day of activities. Unfortunately, since it is still quite light outside at this late hour-- especially in view of the fact that the Finns stay up virtually all night during the summer months--X suggested that we visit a good friend of his who runs a militaria business some 20 km from Lahti. The friend, formerly in the Finnish military, now operates a funeral home during the day and sells military items in his spare time. X described him as a renaissance man, in view of his many unique interests. Truly he was.

We arrived near midnight and spent the next three hours with T. of the InterArmy Company. T. has a most amazing collection of military items, about 78% of which is Russian in origin. Not the run-of-the-mill militaria that is flooding the US market right now but some truly exotic items that you don't find anywhere else: experimental Russian Titanium prototype battle helmets, depth gauges from Russian submarines, sensitive avionics from Russian fighter jets, Soviet Spetznast (Special Forces) equipment, antitank weapons, Russian fighter pilot helmets and personal equipment, etc., etc. The list is endless and all are for sale, except for the crème de la crème of the inventory, which ends up in his personal collection. I promised T. that I would put him in touch with some US collectors and entrepreneurs who might be interested in a retail partnership, and had a few more beers as I marveled over the breadth of these things. T. even had a full sized Russian troop transport truck out in front of the office which he had acquired and was interested in selling.

I was finally able to suggest that we depart and after thanking T. for his hospitality, we headed back to Lahti at about 0300 hours with plenty of twilight still in evidence. The Finns seldom sleep during the long summer months due to the constant sunlight, and this probably compensates somewhat for the equally long winter months in which there is little or any sun at all. For people used to a full 8 hours of sleep each night such as my wife and I, this was starting to become something of a burden.

Early next morning all four of us, X & his wife and I and my own, were up loading the small hatchback with our mutual luggage--not an easy task, given the small size of the car. It was a challenge, but with my years of experience serving as a loadmaster on a VW beetle we managed it. After a huge (typically Finnish) breakfast, we drove down towards Helsinki for one final of sightseeing in the "new" capitol (Turku was the original one, and Helsinki was selected as an expedient to heavy Russian pressure at the end of the war).

Ch. 21. RUSSIAN SUBMARINES & HOT DOGS:

In Helsinki, we arrived at the home of X's sister who lives in a large flat in the city. From there we did the 24-hour concentrated tour of this very unusually modern Scandinavian city. The weather was still sunny, although it threatened rain later in the day, so we had a great dose of taking in all the sights that there are to see. Included in this tour was an inspection of a Russian Juliette-Class nuclear missile submarine, which is now anchored in Helsinki harbor as a temporary display on loan from Russia. X and I must have spent the better part of two hours combing the huge steel tube through from stem to stern in the now increasing drizzle; both of us found it endlessly fascinating, although the wives predictably ho-hummed and fretted over our boyish enthusiasms. This prowl through the multiple-levels of Russia's U-484 revealed many profound differences between their submarines and those of the United States. Their subs are a nightmare of tangled steel conduits and electrical junctions, combined with a nightmarish plumbing setup that would make an Ubanetsky modern painting look aesthetically understandable. It must be mentioned that the Juliette-class boats are the only type of submarine in the whole world that were designed and developed by a woman marine architect (with a NATO identifier of "Juliette," who says NATO had no sense of humor during the worst days of the Cold War?). Strangely, despite this fact, there were no signs over the heads reminding the crew to put the seats down after use...

The drizzle, which had just started when we reached the U-484, began to increase to the point where it was raining quite considerably so I was unable to get more than one or two poor photographs of it from the dock across from it. Some wag operating the submarine museum concession had run a bright red KOFF beer flag up the periscope shears, right under the old Soviet red naval ensign. It made for an amusing if somewhat unglamorous counternote to the exhibit of this interesting old survivor of frigid deep-water intrigues. After buying some hot dogs by the gang-plank leading to the sub's hatch, we were told that a gourmet dinner could be arranged by special request in the sub's officer's mess; catering for groups of less than 12 could be provided to constitute what has to be one of the world's more unusual opportunities for an evening's dining at a decidedly unconventional submersible restaurant. That would have to rank as an exotic experience on the short list of such things, considering not just the location of the dinner but the cramped space available aboard the boat. The U-484's four nuclear tipped cruise-type guided missiles, carried in firing tubes hidden in the upper deck casing, had been removed, naturally enough, but it was sobering enough just to see the cavernous recesses in the launch area where they were stowed. Just before leaving, X and I got a few pictures of each other posing at the main periscope in true dramatic war-movie style. So much for grown up children and their fantasies, eh?

The distaff element of our group was starting to mumble about a possible mutiny, so X and I reluctantly left this great big, 3000-ton plaything for some more mutually agreeable sightseeing. At present, word has it that Helsinki is negotiating with the Russian Navy for loan of a Typhoon-class nuclear submarine. The U-484 has a displacement of 3500 tons; the Typhoon-class subs, which are nuclear powered and carried as many as 16 intercontinental nuclear missiles, weigh in at over 12,500 tons! This compared to a German World War Two Atlantic U-boat, such as the Type VIIC, which weighed a mere 750 tons. The old saying has it that the only difference between the men and the boys is the cost of their toys. I would amend that to 'the size of their toys," as well. How about something like that in your bath-tub?

Ch. 22. ARABIAN TOILETS IN HELSINKI:

Helsinki has quite a lot to see, obviously. The sights were many, the markets and waterfront vendors plentiful and colorful, and we would be exhausted by the time the day was at an end. Among the places visited was the famous Arabia ceramics and porcelain factory with all its exquisite glass and art objects. The factory showroom, where all their samples and seconds are sold, must have been to our wives what the Juliette-class was for X and I. I had to admit that their products are beautiful, well known throughout the world for artful style and craftsmanship. I was vastly amused to find that every toilet in Finland (they seem all to be manufactured by the Arabia Company) has the word "ARABIA" scribed on its flushing knob. This was a note of irony I particularly enjoyed, considering how frequently I have used excremental terms to describe my feelings on how it is to have to live with the Arabs.

Our wandering took us from the Arabia factory to the downtown center where we had lunch in the Happy Days bar and restaurant in the waterfront's nearby park-square. A strange mixture of American 60s bizarre style and Finnish pop eclecticism, it was strangely appealing in an otherwise urban sylvan setting where drunks sat propped up against tree trunks in a harmless but sad manner that seemed perfectly normal. X remarked that Finnish alcoholism is still a major problem, but not as bad as it once used to be.

Ch. 23. GERMAN SUBMARINES & CHI-
NESE FOOD:

The final act of this last day was to visit the *Island Fortress of Suomelinen* which contains all sorts of interesting sights. Among these are the very old fortifications of the original island defense works, established many, many years ago to protect the harbor, a number of maritime displays, and what for X and I was the major draw: the *submarine Vesikko.*

Vesikko, is a very interesting old submarine which began its life as a prototype of Germany's new Kriegsmarine, designed and ordered by Germany before the war (in the 1930s). It was built by Finnish industries and was then purchased by the Finnish Navy as the first-of-5 similar craft to be operated during the war. The Vesikko was very similar to the so-called German Coastal U-boat (Type IIB) in size and displacement (about 350 tons), but bears remarkable resemblance to the famous Atlantic U-boat Type VIIC which was responsible for most of the allied shipping losses during the war. It was, practically speaking, an advance product of Germany's cover gearing up for what became the Second World War, in contravention of the terms of the First World War's armistice.

Another submarine to explore! Boy, were X and I happy! The girls, as could be predicted, were far from happy crewmates on this sub-crawl and once again the smell of a mutiny brewed up after we had had only a brief time to inspect this latest bath-tub super-toy. Reluctantly, X and I left the Vesikko where she rests, high and dry on a pedestal near the water, and resumed our exploration of some of the rest of the island.

This brought the total number of submarine explored to three for this trip, since we had found another one in Stockholm Harbor tied up to a dock near the Vaasa Museum. That one had been a conventional electric/diesel boat of the Russian Whiskey-class, designated the U-194. It had been in active use by the Russian Navy since 1957 to prowl Swedish coastal waters, and was kept in service until about 1991, amazingly. The Juliette-class nuclear cruise missile sub in Helsinki Harbor (U-484) had been in use by Russia until 1994!

Finally, late in the evening, my wife and I hosted X and his wife at a fairly good Chinese restaurant in the old port area of the Helsinki waterfront. While nothing to write the relatives back in Hong Kong about, it wasn't too bad and X and his wife enjoyed the chance to experience a cuisine which Finns rarely partake of. Arriving back at X's sister's flat quite late, we were really tired, having seen far more than we really had the energy to in this lightning tour of a city that has much to see and experience. Included were the Finnish Modern Art Museum, the very old (second oldest to Turku) city of Pouro with its ancient wooden buildings and the magnificent cathedral, the Helsinki Marimeko Store, the Helsinki University Hospital, the old Helsinki maritime district, and the Finnish Museum of Traditional and Modern arts & Crafts.

The next day we were due to fly out for home, my wife for the US and I for Riyadh. X and his wife would continue their 6-week summer vacation with a trip by car across the Bothnian Gulf to Sweden and Norway, after our departure. We put my wife on her BA 737-400 flight to Heathrow in the early morning, and then X and his wife saw me off on my BA Airbus 300 flight back to Riyadh that afternoon.

My wife was glad to get back to the dogs, both of which she told me were terribly excited to see her after the absence of only a week [It is something else to watch two well-fed Siberian Huskies express their pent-up happiness to be reunited with their humans again after a period of separation.... we're talking "slurp-city."], but she admitted to being somewhat burned out from the strains of having to communicate in such a constantly painstaking manner. I also was feeling the stress of the protracted communication requirement, but I had enjoyed myself thoroughly thanks to X's excellent efforts to provide a visit worth remembering. I was begrudgingly ready for another long, hot, dry and boring as hell summer in Riyadh, but only barely, after having been overwhelmed by Finland's vast green beauty and her wonderfully hospitable inhabitants.

The 3-hour leg of the flight back to Heathrow from Helsinki was uneventful, but the three-hour layover there was infinitely dull. The flight from Heathrow to King Khalid International Airport in Riyadh was also uneventful except for the fact that a small baby being carried to the plane's toilet in its father's arms chose to projectile vomit all over me everything it had eaten in the past several hours. Fortunately for me and the continued survival of the baby, it wasn't a direct hit and I had only a few fleeting urges to strangle it by its little neck before I was able to relax after a bit of reflection on the little pooper's apparent lack of finesse in choosing an appropriate target.

The unavoidable ordeal of clearing Saudi customs wasn't half as bad as I had expected and shortly after the arrival of our flight at 0600 hours Riyadh time I was waved through and caught a taxi back to the hospital compound. I was carrying some 6 kilos of printed material, brochures, papers, magazines and what-have-you from the NBC conference in Stockholm and the weeks spent with the Finns. When the customs inspector saw all of this he simply gave up trying to inspect it all for illicit "nasty" pictures. For my part, I couldn't believe I had managed to lug all that stuff home with me; even the framed photo of the two Drakens in flight over Tampere had survived the flight, with glass intact.

The trip had been overall one of the best I have taken in recent years, and was certainly genuinely enjoyable and interesting. My wife was pleased with introduction to these two Scandinavian countries, despite the wearying pace and breadth of the trip.

X and his wife, by the way, are planning to spend several weeks with my wife and I in the coming year and we shall be returning the favor of hospitality. My wife will show X's wife the sights and scenes of California while I take X on a tour of the defense establishments. He is looking forward to that as I am.

I expect X and I are an excellent illustration of the old saying about scratching the man and find the boy within. Well hell, X and I shall have a whole new set of war toys to play with shortly, when he arrives in the US. Watch out, Robert Bly; here we come, and don't ever forget Rule Number One!

EPILOGUE:

(On the strange and sad fate of Russian submarine U-484.)

A Cold Warrior's Final Patrol: Russian Submarine K-77 (Juliet Class U-484)

March 2010, the annual Hollywood *Academy Awards* event was held amidst all the splashy *hoopla-de-da* that characterises this recurrent self-celebration of *tinsel town's* best creative efforts. I don't normally pay much attention to all the fluff and attendant media fawning therein, but the Oscar awards ceremony this year was markedly different for the following reason: for the very first time in motion picture history a woman was awarded Oscars for *both* 'Best Director' and 'Best Film'. [What *didn't* happen, but perhaps should have, is a special award of *'Best Supporting Submarine'* to the ex-Soviet *Juliet Class* boat that starred in another of Bigelow's earlier films (but more about that later).]

As anyone who follows film media knows, Hollywood has traditionally been a supreme bastion of entrenched male chauvinism and women, except on rare occasions (when raw talent has trumped gender associations), have typically been regarded at best as little more than intelligent sex-objects. Consequent with Kathryn Bigelow's commendable (and in my opinion, much deserved) double Oscar win, I personally sat up and took serious note of this attractive 59-year-old woman's list of past cinematic accomplishments. I was amazed and surprised to learn that she had been the director of that unusual, but outstandingly quirky film 'Point Break' featuring a couple of California surfers who rob a bank (wearing masks of US presidents), but I was further fascinated to find she had also directed one of my favorite war films, a Harrison Ford Cold War epic titled 'K-19: The Widowmaker' (based on an actual unfortunate Echo-2 Class Soviet nuclear missile submarine that sustained a near-meltdown of its nuclear pile while on war patrol).

Cut to April of 2007, at which time a Russian submarine sank to the bottom of the Providence River, while moored to a wharf in Rhode Island. Regrettably, it remained there for just over a full year while efforts were made to determine how to raise the 4,000-ton vessel from its watery resting place at Collier Point Park. The amazing story of how Soviet submarine K-77 came to its final end in the United States, after surviving 27 years of the 'Cold War' as a Soviet guided missile submarine followed by an additional 17 years out of active commission as a warship (serving as a museum display), and how it relates to the film *'K-19: The Widowmaker'*, constitutes a most interesting and surprising saga.

THE SOVIET 'PODNODVAYA LODKA RAKETNAYA KRYLATAYA' SUBMARINES

Soviet submarine K-77 began its life in a ship-builder's yard located in Nizhny Novgorod, Russia, the seventh *Juliet Class* boat built among its 16 Juliet Class sister subs between 1963 and 1968. While the name 'Juliet' is an arbitrary NATO imposed Cold War era identification assigned to K-77's class, its selection in this reference reflects a somewhat curious and unknown aspect of these boats in that they were the first submarine vessels designed principally by a (Russian) *woman* naval architect. Officially recorded in Russian naval archives as the 'Project 651' hull K-77 submarine, this *Cruise Missile Attack* type sub's keel was laid on January 31st of 1963. The boat was commissioned on 31 October 1965 and during its service carried an original war load of twenty-two regular torpedoes and four Soviet P-5 nuclear tipped cruise missiles stowed in special launch tubes built into its outer, upper hull structure. The Juliet Class boats had been initially conceived as a post-war offensive addition to the Soviet Navy's weapons arsenal that would give the Soviet Union the ability to launch cruise missiles (with nuclear warheads) against the seaboard cities of the United States. The concept would later grow to embrace the use of more advanced cruise missiles against American aircraft carriers (so-called *super-carriers*), since the Soviets had no such vessels and American carriers (with their great strategic mobility and airpower assets) were viewed as a grave threat to the USSR in the event that the *cold war* suddenly turned hot.

The P-5 turbojet-propelled (albeit augmented by two solid-fuel rocket launch boosters) missile initially carried by the Juliet Class boats was a relatively short-range weapon (300 miles) carrying a 2,000-pound nuclear payload at an altitude of from 600 to 1300 feet, but these were later replaced by upgraded P-6 and P-500 cruise missiles with extended range and capabilities. Although as originally conceived, the Soviet plan called for more than 75 of these conventionally powered (diesel and electric motor propulsion) missile carrying vessels to be built, that number was eventually trimmed down to a total of only 35, of which 16 were eventually built. Since a larger and more powerfully armed version of the type known as the Echo-2 Class (with nuclear powered propulsion and *eight* cruise missile launchers) were already being built, the advantages offered by nuclear propulsion for extended global operations seemed to offset a larger conventionally powered class.

Considered to be an aesthetically attractive submarine design, the Juliet Class boats proved in service to be basically well engineered and operationally quite reliable, whereas their larger nuclear-powered sister class (Project 675, *Echo-2*) relatives were to demonstrate recurrent, severe design problems with their nuclear propulsion units in succeeding years, frequently developing many near catastrophic faults while underway and on patrol.

As was the case regarding many of both the US and Soviet submarine designs produced in the aftermath of the Second World War, the strong influence of late wartime German submarine research and development made itself apparent in new boats like the K-77. A comparison of the 3174-ton displacement (surfaced) K-77 with wartime U-boats (such as those represented by the substantially advanced German Type XXI) clearly shows the lineage of their German-derived technology. This advanced technology came to serve both the Russian and American sides as part of the massive post-war recovery of German advanced research in weapons systems, and just as German aircraft breakthroughs formed the foundation of most US and Russian advances in aeronautical engineering, so did WWII German naval research significantly further the development

of modern submarine fleets on both sides of
the *Iron Curtain*.

The Juliet Class boats were fitted with (at the time)
sophisticated weapons aiming and targeting radar
systems that were intended for use in precisely
guiding the P-5 missiles to their selected targets.
Although the primary guidance system employed
on board the Soviet cruise missiles was inertial, a
massive (over 100 square feet) directional guidance
radar antenna built into the forward part of the
Juliette's sail (or *conning tower*), was used to send
mid-course corrections to the missiles while in
flight. Hidden behind a large hydrodynamically
streamlined section of faired forward sail plating,
the radar antenna was rotated 180 degrees from its
'stowed' facing aft just before launch—a process
that took several minutes once the boat had
surfaced. This radar guidance system was later
down-linked to the Soviet *Kasatka* satellite
communications network when more advanced
missiles came into use (P-6 and P-500), allowing
more precise aiming and directional targeting
uplinks to the launched missiles.

Although the first two Juliet Class boats had been
constructed from special low-magnetic
signature *austenitic steel*, a number of serious
problems resulted from its use with the result that
K-77's hull was fabricated from conventional steel.

K-77's hull was further coated with a two-inch layer of sound deadening polymeric (specially profiled and formulated acoustic rubber) tiles that made the Juliet Class boats a somewhat formidable threat to US warships in the late 60s period. Despite a general tendency for Russian submarines of that era to be excessively noisy while submerged and therefore easily picked up on sonar, the Juliet Class vessels operated in markedly silent contrast to that otherwise norm for Soviet boats, and although the relatively short range of their missiles was a limiting factor, the offensive threat they posed could never be fully dismissed out of hand.

The primary vulnerability of the Juliet Class lay in the fact that the missiles had to be launched from the surface (at a maximum forward speed of about 4-5 knots). Since the total time required from surfacing to actual firing was in excess of 5 minutes, the threat posed by the Juliet Class boats was gradually downgraded by the West, as it was felt that in any genuine' hot war' scenario, the boats would likely have been detected and destroyed by US defense forces before they could get off their first cruise missile salvo. This inherent vulnerability of the Juliet and Echo-2 subs was further enhanced by the fact that they had to remain on the surface for as long as 20 minutes *after* launch, so as to be able to radar-track and guide the deployed missiles. Under such circumstances, it would have been imperative that the Juliet and Echo-2 subs have an active air cover umbrella in the form of fighter planes for their effectiveness to be assured.

Although the improved Echo-2 nuclear powered boats were equally vulnerable in their missile launch cycle (despite possessing the advantage of nuclear propulsion), the Soviet Naval Command kept the newer Echo-2 boats operating globally while the slightly smaller and conventionally powered Juliets were redirected from former global strategic patrol duties (shadowing enemy carriers and lurking close-in to enemy coastal cities) to supportive duty with the Soviet Baltic Fleet.
In terms of their physical and operating specifications, the following technical facts associated with the Juliet Class boats are worth noting, at this point.

JULIETT CLASS SUBMARINE SPECIFICATIONS

Build Specs: Length = 300 feet. Beam = 33 feet. Displacement = 3,174 tons (without fuel) surfaced and 4,137 tons submerged, with an exceptionally large reserve buoyancy engineered into the double hull. The upper free-flooding outer hull was also unusually capacious and large enough to stow the four missiles within its structure.
Propulsion: Conventional diesel/electric, with two main D-43 type diesel engines providing 3500 HP

each and two electric motors yielding 3000 HP each. An additional ultra-silent running capability was enabled through use of a special set of smaller electric engines, each with an output of 150 HP. 300 tons of conventional electrical storage batteries were used (initially silver/zinc, but later reverted to standard lead/acid), along with a 3000 HP dedicated 2D-42 diesel powered generator to charge them while running on the surface *or* submerged (a modern Soviet version of the German *'Schnorkel'* system was used by the Juliet Class boats while at sea, enabling them to operate submerged on diesel engines). Although helpful for avoiding detection, submerged diesel operation with the snorkel was a taxing, exhausting (no pun intended) undertaking and sailing on a Juliet Class boat was therefore far more arduous for crews than serving on the entirely self-contained and nuclear-powered Echo-2 Class relatives.

Performance (speed/range): 17 knots surfaced, 18 submerged. Patrol endurance was about 90 days, with a crew complement of 64 (including 12 officers and 16 Petty Officers) and range was generally about 9000 miles surfaced (at 8 knots) and about 810 miles submerged (at 3 knots).

Armament: Primary offensive weaponry included four P-5, P-6, or P-500 (SS-N-3 'Shaddock') turbojet powered, booster rocket-assist launched nuclear tipped cruise missiles with a range of about 300 miles. Secondary weaponry included six bow torpedo tubes and 4 stern tubes (loaded with anti-submarine torpedoes), with a total of 18 to 22 dual-purpose torpedoes (acoustic active/passive warheads).

Missile guidance system: Internally inertially directed and radar corrected, with later *Kasatka* satellite guidance capability added, using the *'Snoop Slab'* or *'Snoop Tray'* (both NATO designations) I-band radar to provide mid-flight course modification commands.

With eight integrated watertight main compartments and three floor levels within the inner pressure hull, the Juliet boats were strongly constructed and had a 'test depth' (generally considered their normal 'safe' diving depth) of approximately of 775 feet, a design depth of about 1200 feet, and an absolute crush depth of 1350 feet. It is noteworthy that of all 16 Juliet Class boats built and commissioned from 1963 through 1968, not one was lost in sea-going operations and all were eventually retired and decommissioned, the last one serving satisfactorily until 1994.

DEPLOYMENT AND OPERATIONAL SERVICE

Of the 16 Juliets, six boats were originally assigned to the Soviet Northern Fleet, while another six were assigned for use by the Baltic and Black Sea Fleets (to be split between them). Four boats were assigned to the Soviet Pacific Fleet (documentation notes that in 1987, the six Northern Fleet boats were reassigned to the Baltic Fleet).

The missiles carried by both Juliet and Echo-2 Classes deserve a bit of further description here, since they were of the early air-breathing cruise type weapon configuration that came into use prior to development of more powerful and precise sub-surface launched ballistic missiles. Both the United States and the Soviet Union developed air-breathing, submarine launched cruise missiles in the years immediately following the war and both nations based their systems on the German V-1 ramjet-powered winged missile developed in the last half of the war and used against English cities, along with the ballistic, rocket powered V-2 missile.

In the USA, this took the form of the *Loon* (a V-1 clone), the *Regulus I*, and *Regulus II* missiles. With a range of about 250 nautical miles, their original Soviet counterpart, the P-5 (SS-N-3c 'Pityorka', AKA 'Shaddock') was used on converted ('Long Bin') Whiskey Class (conventional diesel/electric), Juliet Class (also conventional), and Echo-2 Class (nuclear powered) Soviet submarines. They used a folded-wing configuration that allowed them to be stored within a clever tubular launcher that could be stowed within the outer, upper (non-pressurised) hull of a sub and fired after being erected to a 35-degree launch position. Similar in concept to a US *Regulus* missile, the P-5 missile used a turbojet air intake below the cylindrical main body of the missile and was configured with a clipped delta tail-plane, provided with two moving control surfaces, and incorporated twin 1750-pound solid rocket booster rockets that were discarded shortly after launch.

The P-5 missile was designed to fly at an altitude varying between three hundred and a thousand, three-hundred feet, reaching a cruising speed of about .9 Mach (just slightly above the speed of a modern commercial airliner, or about 600 mph). Capable of penetrating US coastal defense of the early 60s, the P-5 missile had a circular target error at full range of about 9000 feet, but made up for this rather flawed accuracy by virtue of its 2090 pound 'RDS-4' nuclear warhead. The Juliet Class's P-5 and succeeding P-6 missiles used the same basic procedure as the US Navy's submarine launched Regulus missile of surface launch, with loitering in a surfaced state being required to provide continuous tracking and course correction inputs to target.

The improved P-6 (SS-N-3a 'Progress', AKA 'Shaddock') missile had the same range as the earlier P-5, but achieved a slightly higher cruise speed of about 1.2 Mach *en route* to the target. As with its predecessor, the P-6 was vulnerable to both air-intercept by aircraft and ECM jamming. The P-500 (with 4K-80 nuclear warhead) series cruise missile, last to be used on the Juliet Class boats, was a dedicated anti-ship weapon with much improved guidance, speed and electronics and intended principally to take out US super-carriers.

Juliette Class boats were spotted in a number of places about the globe during their several decades of operation, from their initial deployment up through the 80s and early 90s. Frequently detected shadowing the US super carriers they were assigned to take out in the event of a hot war, Juliets put in regular appearances in the North Atlantic and Mediterranean oceans. A small flotilla of Juliets were also used as escorts for a Soviet guided missile frigate in the Tonkin Gulf at one point, which appeared in those waters as a reminder to the United States of the not-to-be-underestimated presence of Soviet naval might near Vietnam.

THE END OF THE COLD WAR AND DECOMMISSIONING

K-77, also known more popularly as *Juliet 484*, was initially assigned to duty with the Soviet Northern Fleet, operating on the shores of the Barents Sea near the Kola Peninsula. When the Soviet Union officially came to an end (with the establishment of the Russian Federation in 1990), K-77 was one of two ex-Soviet submarines of her class that were stationed in reserve status at the former Soviet Naval Base of *Liepaja* on the coast of Latvia, along with two boats of the diesel/electric *Foxtrot Class* and several other Russian naval surface vessels.

It was a time of great political, social, and economic turmoil for the new Russian state, as Russia suddenly found itself possessed of ponderously expensive and over-extended military forces, obsolete armament (much of it now outmoded by more recent advancements) and millions of unneeded military personnel that it had built up during the Cold War period. With the Cold War now officially ended, the newly emergent economic reality demanded extreme austerity from the Russian Republic, requiring many painful cuts and eventual reductions in both its military forces and surplus materiel.

Among the suddenly 'expendable' Russian defense items at the *Leipaja* base in Latvia were the two Juliette Class boats wharved at the former Soviet naval anchorage. These two boats were the K-77 (AKA: *Juliet 484*) and a sister boat, the K-24 (AKA: *Juliet 461*), which had been assigned to the Soviet Baltic Fleet. Although the Juliets were taken briefly out of service by the Soviet Navy in the early 80s, they had been placed back in service in 1985; two of the fleet ended up in reserve status, due to certain strategic arms limitations stipulations. The two *Leipaja* Juliets were eventually decommissioned in 1994.

With Latvia demanding immediate return of the *Leipaja* anchorage to their nation, the Russian Navy now faced a rather uncomfortable dilemma: how to dispose of some of their large number of submarines (both conventionally powered and nuclear), now that the base they were tied up at belonged to the Latvian Republic? It was a perplexing challenge, since the logistical considerations (particularly with reference to the nuclear-powered subs, with their potentially hazardous propulsion plants) were as enormous as the economic ones. Meanwhile, the two Juliets simply sat at their dock, gathering rust. As may be easily recognised, disposing of nuclear submarines carries substantial risks due to their nuclear propulsion systems and the possibilities contained therein for dangerous and extremely hazardous contamination; conventionally powered submarines with their electric/diesel engines, on the other hand, are inherently less environmentally hazardous by an order of magnitude.

At this point, an unusual sequence of events occurred. A Finnish businessman named Jari Komulainen, who had been visiting *Leipaja* (Latvia), spotted the two Juliets at anchor and had a most unusual idea. Surely some of the two ex-Soviet subs could be made into fascinating 'Cold War' floating museums for the Finnish people and foreign visitors to Helsinki to enjoy? Since Finland had been forbidden to build or operate submarines at the end of the war (due to their alliance with Nazi Germany), and mindful of Finland's earlier association with the *Vesikko* (a prototype for the World War Two German Type II Class submarine, built for Finland in 1933, now on permanent land-based display on Suomenlinna island in Helsinki Harbor as part of the Finnish Military Museum), Komulainen approached the commercial attaché at the Russian embassy in Helsinki and proposed that he be allowed to personally purchase one or two of the surplus Juliette Class boats for this purpose.

By a gratifying coincidence, the Russian *attaché* was a former submarine

commander who had earlier helped Komulainen
obtain one of the conventionally powered ex-Soviet
Foxtrot Class boats (Project 641 submarine) in
1993. Quickly perceiving the novel value of such an
arrangement, not to mention the convenience factor
embodied in what amounted to a very clever way of
disposing of two obsolete, surplus-to-need
submarines for his government, he was agreeable
to the proposal; eventually both the K-77 and her
sister Juliet Class boat (the K-24) were acquired by
Komulainen for use as public displays.

While the K-24 went initially to Copenhagen for
dockside exhibition (and later to the German
Maritime Museum at Peenemunde, where it
remains on display today), K-77 was soon towed to
Helsinki Harbor and installed at a wharf there, near
the shipyards. Aside from the novelty of having a
former undersea Russian warship open for
inspection, the close interactions of Finland and
Russia (more often extremely antagonistic than not
over the past 100 years) had cultivated a further
fascination among the Finns for this relic of the
Cold War. By 1994, the ex-Soviet Foxtrot Class sub
was gone and replaced by the K-77, which was
pressed into initial use as an off-beat floating bar &
restaurant. For this purpose, two large cuts had
been made into the pressure hull allowing a less
restricted general access to the sub's interior (these
large openings were secured by *dogged* doors, but

they were not of the pressure-resistant, watertight variety, a fact would have later significance when K-77 sank at dockside in Rhode Island in 2007, as shall be seen). [Note: Regrettably, the Project 641 Foxtrot Class boat that K-77 had replaced was shortly thereafter lost at sea while under tow to a future display venue in England.]

Originally known as K-77, the name *'Juliet U-484'* was acquired by the boat while she remained as a tourist attraction in Helsinki. According to Komulainen, the designation had been found inscribed on a plate uncovered within the craft's sail. The designation seems to have been one of a number of removable designations the K-77's crew used to display on the sail's exterior while on patrol so as to confuse and throw off NATO reconnaissance aircraft. Before long, the 'U' component in the name was dropped and she remained simply 'Juliet 484'.

According to an October 2002 article by Sami Soininen in the *Helsingin Sanomat* newspaper, K-77 was not the source of inordinate profit for entrepreneur Komulainen that he may have originally envisioned, but it did remain at least *somewhat* profitable. The boat remained a singular draw for a wide range of people including native Finns as well as foreign visitors (who would first see the Juliet Class boat and then take a ferry

to nearby Suomenlinna to view the
famous *Vesikko* Type II U-boat precursor). Former
submarine service officers of all nationalities were
invariably attracted to K-77 and 'Juliette 484'
became quite a well-known aspect of Helsinki's
many charming attractions.

During her years at Helsinki, there were a number
of unusual inquiries by strange groups and
individuals asking if the boat were for sale. One of
these, we are told by journalist Soininen, was a
cartel of Arabs from an unnamed Middle Eastern
nation who seriously wanted to put the boat back
into sea-going condition (for unknown purposes—
one can only imagine). Another equally shadowy
group turned out to be of Columbian (South
America) nationality and although their offer to
purchase the submarine was refused, American
DEA agents later revealed that the Columbians
were members of the infamous *Cali Cartel* who
wanted a submarine for use in their drug-smuggling
operations (despite their failure in obtaining this, or
any other former military submarine, the Cali cartel
today employs a number of much smaller, home-
made submersible craft for this purpose).

Visual examination of K-77 close-up by American
Naval authorities confirmed what had already been
discovered back in the 1970s by US sonar experts,
that concave sections of the Juliet Class boat's

upper hull (designed to act as missile launch exhaust ducts) caused a distinctively singular sonar signature, thereby making identification of submerged Juliet Class boats a fairly simple matter for US anti-submarine forces of that era. This liability, combined with the unavoidable surface exposure required for launch and guidance of the *Shaddock* missiles, rendered the class technologically obsolete long before they were actually decommissioned. The surmise by US submarine warfare experts is that the Juliet Class boats, while essentially useless in the often shallow and rocky coastal operating areas of the Scandinavian nations (where only smaller, shallower draft submarines could operate with reasonable safety), would have been best employed in support of Soviet nuclear capabilities in the Baltic Sea. Despite that supposition, among the many paper documents found still on board the boat (surprisingly) when it was sold to Komulainen were several that suggested the boat had at some time been shadowing Norwegian *Kobben Class* submarines at some point in its operational history.

In 1997, which is when I was taking a tour of Finnish defense facilities as a guest of the Finnish Defense Ministry, one of the side-excursions we made was to examine K-77. It was a very, very overcast day when we drove down to the harbor and I well recall seeing the darkened hull of this clearly Russian designed submarine looming out of the water at dockside like some sort of sinister sea-monster; it made quite an impression on me at the time. Flying from one of its periscopes was the blue, white and red Soviet Naval Ensign as we approached its berth and flying from another was the Communist red hammer and sickle flag (inappropriately, since Soviet subs *never* flew that flag in active service); we subsequently spent a good two hours going over the boat from stem to stern—an inspection I very much relished. Little did I dream I'd soon be seeing the same interior spaces once more in Hollywood director Kathryn Bigelow's film *'K-19: The Widowmaker'* and not recognise them! I managed to shoot two rolls of film within K-77's interior and out on its deck, but to my everlasting regret left one of the exposed rolls sitting on a charting table in the control room!

K-77 COMES TO AMERICA AND BECOMES A HOLLYWOOD CELEBRITY

Shortly after my visit K-77's tenure as a museum display boat in Helsinki Harbor came to an end when Komulainen managed to lease the submarine to a Canadian promoter as a tourist destination in St. Petersburg, Florida. After an uneventful tow across the Atlantic, the boat arrived at St. Petersburg only to find that given the sub's fairly deep draft, its intended mooring site there was too shallow (the sub draws over about 27 feet at the stern). This necessitated moving it to a more distant location where tourist access was somewhat hampered. Due to lowered tourist visits, before long the Canadian promoter was forced to declare bankruptcy and after a brief effort to sell the submarine on eBay (with a price tag of a million US dollars, in 1999) ownership of K-77 once more reverted to Komulainen. Wishing to get the aging submarine out of its harbor, where it was regarded as a possible hurricane hazard, Komulainen did not want to undergo the cost and difficulty of having the sub towed back across the Atlantic to Finland. Fortunately, at this time *Intermedia Films*, in cooperation with the *National Geographic Foundation*, was about to undertake the filming of a movie to be titled *'K-19: The Widowmaker'*. Starring Harrison Ford and Liam Neeson and directed by now well-known and Oscar winning director Kathryn Bigelow, the film was based on the story of a Soviet Hotel Class nuclear submarine (K-19) that experienced a catastrophic nuclear reactor meltdown while on its maiden voyage in 1961. Over 20 crew members died as a result of that incident and although the sub was eventually decontaminated and returned to service, it forever after acquired the nickname *Hiroshima* among Soviet submarine crews. Word of the boat's availability had apparently reached the film's producers in Hollywood, subsequent to all the publicity arising from its attempted sale on eBay.

Intermedia therefore expressed an interest in acquiring temporary use of K-77 for its film and shortly after an agreed-upon one-year rental of about $200,000.00 had been paid, the sub was towed up to Halifax, Nova Scotia, where some structural modification was undertaken on its hull (for the film). Per Soininen's account, K-77's hull was lengthened by some 25 feet and its superstructure was slightly modified to resemble a Hotel Class nuclear submarine. Interestingly, the involvement of the National Geographic group resulted in an insistence that absolute accuracy in depiction of a Hotel Class boat (which was a nuclear ballistic missile submarine) be maintained as much as possible...evidence of the fact that the old Hollywood technique of using underwater shots of a US WWII Fleet Type boat for *ALL* films about submarines had long since come to an end (fortunately!).

We are further told that due to restricted space inside K-77, major portions of the boat were removed and reconstructed in sound-stage sets on shore where filming could be more easily accomplished. An agreement signed by all parties involved in the film stipulated that when filming of the movie was finished, the boat would be returned to its original, pre-movie state. In order to assure this, over 1000 still photographs and a number of detailed drawings were undertaken prior to the modifications required.

After the year required for filming expired, the same problem as before presented itself once more: what to do with a very large, outsized and difficult to dock former Soviet submarine? Halifax port authorities were as anxious as their counterparts in St. Petersburg to see the huge 3174-ton submarine relocated to another site and the requirement for a fairly deep-water berth for the boat proved again to be an effective deterrent for most potential buyers. Once again, K-77 faced the prospect of being an unwanted behemoth orphan in the storm and it was anyone's guess as to what the boat's fate might have been (sold prematurely for salvage as scrap?), had it not have been for a group in Rhode Island calling itself the *USS Saratoga Museum Foundation*.

USS SARATOGA FOUNDATION TO THE RESCUE

The USS Saratoga Foundation is based at the former US Naval Air Station at Quonset Point, RI, and its declared goal was to turn the facility into a theme-oriented naval park with the 56,000-ton *Forrestal Class* super-carrier as its principal focus. Interestingly, the Saratoga had been decommissioned in 1994 (the same year that K-77 had been taken out of Soviet service) and the prospect of having a former Soviet super-carrier killer submarine to serve as a storied counterfoil to the mighty Saratoga was undeniably attractive to many. The idea that the Saratoga and other large American Forrestal Class aircraft carriers of its type had been the principal targets of Juliet Class subs was hard to resist and it almost seemed like a natural for the foundation to add K-77 to its park, for use as a Cold War era floating museum.

Owing to the fact that the Saratoga was still US Navy property and the fact that the foundation had not yet convinced the navy that its Quonset Point venue was the proper final resting place for the great carrier, the president of the Saratoga Foundation felt that having the K-77 on display would serve the additional purpose of acting as a powerful marketing incentive, furthering broad support for the Saratoga acquisition proposal. With a Board of Advisors comprised of a number of retired former US naval officers of elevated rank and with a large and enthusiastic volunteer base of former navy volunteers and general members (reportedly over 4000), it seemed as if there would be a substantial financial support base to draw upon for both K-77's and the Saratoga's acquisition. Negotiations were therefore initiated with

Komulainen to acquire K-77 for this purpose and after an unspecified asking price was paid (reckoned to be about $500,000 or less), the sub was once again towed by sea from Halifax to its new berth at Quonset Point. The new Saratoga Museum Foundation museum sub formally opened in 2002.

A careful search of the K-77's interior compartments after the boat had been handed over revealed a further extensive cache of overlooked documents, photographs, radio messages, and maintenance reports (all in Russian, of course) that had apparently been left behind when the submarine was originally been sold to Komulainen in 1993. The most important finding from this unexpected trove of data was that K-77 was *indeed* K-77 and *not* K-81, as has been erroneously claimed by several sources on the internet. As part of the initial work, the Saratoga Foundation also began efforts to get in touch with former Soviet Navy submariners who had sailed on K-77 and learned that the boat had patrolled in the Mediterranean Sea, been in coastal waters of West Africa and on patrol off the US Virgin Islands. Of further interest was the information that once during her years of service, there had been a fire on board that had killed two of her crew. *Ghosts* on the K-77? *Perhaps.*

Given that the K-77 is an immense and ponderous vessel (one of the largest non-nuclear submarines ever built) drawing about 23 - 29 feet of water, finding a suitable berthing site for her posed special concerns. The boat was eventually tied up on the Providence River at Collier Point Park, a site adjacent to the former Quonset Point Naval Air Station. Although the river at that site has a sloping bank gradient, the boat was moored parallel to shore and far enough from the bank that this factor (the bank gradient) was felt to have been dealt with adequately as tides rose and fell. Thus, K-77 was finally opened to the public after a complete assay of it had been completed and necessary accommodations made to comply with public access and safety issues. For five years, subsequent to its formal opening in 2002 K-77 served as a fascinating focal point for the Saratoga Foundation's activities and functions, annually drawing a substantial number of interested visitors and providing further incentive for their Saratoga themed park concept to come to ultimate fruition. The large and enthusiastic group of former navy volunteers who support the Saratoga Foundation put in many hours of work on K-77 keeping her shipshape and presentable, no mean feat given the massive maintenance requirements of such a large vessel. It looked as if the benefits of having K-77 on display would continue to serve the Saratoga

Foundation well in its efforts to secure final release of the Saratoga from the US Navy.

MAN PROPOSES, NATURE DISPOSES: THE SAD END OF K-77

Sadly, nature had other ideas and intervened adversely in this plan of the Saratoga Foundation, when Rhode Island was inundated by an unusually severe *"Nor'easter"* storm in April of 2007. In that storm, one of the worst on record, Juliet 484 was swamped by its stern and shortly thereafter sank at its mooring site. Although a formal accident investigation report has yet to be released detailing the *exact* sequence of events that led to this loss, the following events appear to have been primary contributors.

On April 17th, 2007, the storm responsible for K-77's loss had created massive and unusually strong tidal surges in the Providence River. The situation was further complicated by the closing of a special hurricane barrier further up the river and a shift in wind direction to the East (most unusual, per the usually prevailing conditions). When the barrier in question was closed, discharge of redirected water took place in the area very near the sub's stern, creating further abnormally large hydrodynamic surges. This combination of factors apparently resulted in the bow of the sub being pushed inward

toward the shore and the stern being pushed
further out into the river. When the tide dropped that
day, the sub's bow was left aground, while the stern
section fell disproportionately. Due to the fact that
access openings allowing entrance to the aft
torpedo room had been cut into the pressure hull
(when the boat was originally in Finland) and
fitted with hatches that were weather tight but not
pressure/water tight, water began to enter the sub
and gradually filled the aft interior compartment
spaces of the pressure hull.

Although at that point the urgency of the need to
enter the sub and secure internal watertight doors
was clearly recognized, local health and safety
officials prevented museum volunteers from
entering the sub in its semi-flooded state, and there
is little question that the storm was so severe such
actions would have been quite hazardous. Sadly,
the predictable result was that within 30 hours the
entire vessel had filled from stern to bow. The boat
sank to the bottom of the river where it was moored
(water about 35 feet in depth) and given the depth
of the river at that point this left only the periscope
masts above water. The severity of the storm
initially kept anyone from being able to do anything
further at the onset of the emergency, but an
underwater survey of the sunken sub done after the
storm had subsided showed it resting on the river
bottom at a 50-degree list to port, a posture

resulting from dislodged river mud beneath its keel that held the boat there.

Although the Foundation held a one-million-dollar insurance policy on the boat, its provisions stipulated that only half of that amount was eligible for operations involving salvage. Acutely aware of the fact that the longer the sub remained in its sunken exposed status in the river, the less the chances of its being able to be successfully raised and restored, effort nevertheless continued to raise the boat as soon as weather and safety considerations permitted. Months passed, but eventually a cooperative US Army and Navy team effort was able to raise K-77. By the time it was finally brought back to the surface, K-77 had lain on the bottom for just over a full year (15 months) and once the water had finally been pumped out, it quickly became apparent that the damage and exposure was far more extensive than anyone had anticipated. Given the excessive expense that a full restoration effort would have required, the Foundation most reluctantly decided that there was no economically reasonable option to pursue other than to dispose of the boat for its scrap salvage value.

Thus, the boat's remains were sold to the nearby Rhode Island Recycled Metals Corporation (ship breakers) and that company subsequently relocated it to their site not far from the Collier Point Park area. Generously, the agreement reached by RIRM Inc with the museum contained provisions that would make certain components from K-77 available to the Foundation for various purposes directly associated with fund-raising. It is expected that items like K-77's periscopes, torpedo tube doors, missile firing control station, some engine assemblies, and smaller items (like controls and gauges) will serve as saleable artifacts that would help raise money for the Foundation, since these items would have obvious historical value both to museums and collectors. In this manner, despite the sad loss of the entire boat as a complete and historic museum piece itself, at least *portions* of K-77 will survive in private and museum collections. K-77's legacy shall therefore continue in part and memory of her historic role in the Cold War era will not fade away entirely with her loss.

Despite history's having now consigned K-77 to the scrap heap of modern memory, you may still view Oscar winning director Kathryn Bigelow's movie, *K-19: the Widowmaker* (on DVD) and remind yourself that the scenes depicting the Hollywood 'K-19' are actually of K-77. In this manner, although disguised for the movie, K-77 manages to live on in cinematic perpetuity as a final, fitting tribute to her memory. In no small way, both the story of K-77 and Bigelow's movie serve as a further memorial to the thousands of Russian naval officers and seamen who went to sea in the Soviet submarine fleets during the Cold War period.

[Note: Now that 'Juliet 484' has been lost, her sister ship K-24 (Juliet 461) on permanent display at the German Maritime Museum at Peenemunde is the only remaining example of the Juliet Class Soviet submarine left in the entire world. More detailed information on K-24 may be found at the German Maritime Museum's website, given at the end of this article below, and a selection of images of both boats also follows.]

Kalikiano Kalei

ABOUT THE AUTHOR

Kalikiano Kalei is, as are all writers, an accomplished liar. Hence almost nothing he says may be taken at face value or on the assumption that truth is being served. He is the author of several other books on various subjects, a few volumes of tortured poetry, and knows just enough German, Spanish, Hawaiian & Arabic to send their respective peoples running for the hills, screaming! Despite his medical & aviation background, he remains a life-long closet submarine buff.

CPSIA information can be obtained
at www.ICGtesting.com
Printed in the USA
BVOW06*2035070917
R8128000001B/R81280PG493691BVX1B/1/P